1 Why use the target language?

The natural use of the target language for virtually all communication is a sure sign of a good modern language course. National Curriculum Modern Foreign Languages Final Report para 10.7.

Learning a foreign language means acquiring the ability to communicate with people using the language as a tool. The natural place for this communication to begin to take place is within the languages classroom. The use of the target language in the classroom:

- transforms the subject into communication, so that the language is seen as useful now, and not just at some vague point in the future when pupils may go abroad.
- makes the greatest possible use of the time available in the classroom to promote both conscious and subconscious learning. Research in many subjects has shown that we learn most effectively by experiencing and doing; this is particularly true of languages.
- enables pupils to acquire the confidence, para-linguistic skills and coping strategies which, together with their knowledge of the language itself, will equip them to cope effectively in a foreign country.
- enables pupils to relate what they are learning directly to a practical situation, and provides a context in which they can use their new knowledge.
- provides enjoyment, immediate success and motivation for pupils as they realise their ability to communicate with even a limited amount of language.

How can it work for me?

We often overestimate the importance of language in communication. Many of the words we use in our mother tongue are unnecessary and irrelevant. They are often ignored by the people listening to them or reading them, who take note only of the main words. Often meaning is at least partially conveyed by other means. For example:

- The context tells us what people are likely to be saying, or at least it narrows the possibilities.
- Our previous experience of the situation in which we find ourselves combines with the context to give us an idea of what may be said.
- Intonation tells us a lot about the speaker's mood and the general nature of what they are saying.
- Facial expression, hand and body language also convey a lot.

These are things we all use in everyday conversation to convey or understand meaning. As teachers, we can add to this repertoire of aids to meaning, in order to give pupils support in understanding and acquiring language.

How can it work for pupils?

Communication involves not only the teacher but the pupil as well.

Unlike us, pupils don't begin with the necessary language already available. We must provide the language and other skills which they need in order to function fully in the classroom. We must also give them the encouragement, the confidence and the opportunity to use these with success.

2 Will pupils really understand?

The answer to the question is a resounding no, if we speak and write in the target language in exactly the same way as we would in English. In order to ensure understanding, we must look carefully at what we say, how we say it and the support we give to pupils. The success of pupils in understanding is as much our responsibility as theirs, and will only be achieved by our working together with them. This attitude of cooperation in a joint venture should be fostered in pupils, by making sure from the beginning that they have a clear understanding of what we are doing and why, and the part that they can play in this. It is often helpful to relate the process to how they learnt their mother tongue as babies.

The first lessons

The best (but not the only) place to start is right from the first few lessons, as pupils will be enthusiastic and willing to learn, and there will be no need later to undo bad habits. Use short, simple expressions and support everything you say with hand actions, mime or drawings. A thumbs up sign and a smile will convey the meaning of *Très bien/Sehr gut/Molto bene/Muy bien*. Be deliberate in your gestures, even extravagant on occasions. An active and demonstrative style of teaching (jumping up and down or waving your arms in the air) will ensure that your class are watching you. As time goes by, you will be able to revert to a more normal delivery, though your actions and expressions will continue to be important in ensuring comprehension.

Activities

To start with, choose activities which underline the importance for pupils of watching as well as listening. Practise simple instructions with games such as 'Simon Says'. Make sure you are using instructions that are going to be of use later on – *Asseyez-vous, Levez la main, Écoutez* are going to be of more use than *Dansez, Touchez la tête* and *Sautez*. Begin by demonstrating the correct response yourself as you give the instruction, but gradually withdraw this support.

Vocabulary

Teach the vocabulary which pupils are going to need in the classroom. The words for overhead projector, headphones, computer, whiteboard, highlighter should all be included at some stage (see pages 33, 38, 43, 48-9, 54). You may well need to learn some new words yourself. Make sure this vocabulary is added to as pupils use different equipment in language lessons.

Giving oral instructions

As lessons progress, instructions will inevitably become more complicated but they can still be given in the target language if a few simple rules are followed. The important thing, especially at the beginning, is planning. Do not only think about what activities you are going to use but also the language you are going to use to explain them to pupils. You may need to adapt your activities or how you lead up to them in order to take account of this.

Preparation

Is there anything you can prepare beforehand that will make your explanation easier? Drawings, activities involving matching, re-ordering or gap-filling, grids to fill in, true/false statements are just a few ways of avoiding the need for questions in English or complicated explanations in listening and reading tasks. An overhead projector is a great help as all these things can be prepared in advance. In oral activities, if pupils are reading information from a card, then have a larger version available or an overhead projector transparency so that you can point out where the information can be found.

Planning

Is there anything you can do in the early part of the lesson which will lead up to the activity? For example, a group card game can be preceded by a similar game with the whole class using flashcards. This will make your explanation of the group game much easier. A true/false listening activity from a tape could be preceded by a short burst of oral work with some true/false answers, accompanied on the OHP by an illustration of how to record them.

Explanations

What words are you actually going to use to convey the instructions? To begin with, try to indicate the general nature of what is about to happen and what you want the pupils to do. A small set of phrases will be needed which will be used time and time again. Words such as *Travail en groupe, Partnerarbeit, Ascoltate* or *Leed* will soon become familiar to them. Pupils will feel secure in knowing very approximately what they have to do in any particular case, and will have a context in which to work out the rest of the instructions.

Keep it simple

Keep the language involved to a minimum and only say what is necessary. Divide your instructions up into short, easy-to-follow stages and back up each stage with some kind of demonstration. Some words in your instructions will be more important than others, so try to emphasise these, make them louder, follow them or precede them by a pause, or write them on the board. Similarly, some parts of your instructions will be more vital than others. Draw attention to these with phrases such as *Écoutez maintenant* or *Stati attenti*.

Demonstrate

Demonstrate each stage of your instructions as you go along, exaggerating your gestures to make them obvious. Follow up the explanation and demonstration by doing at least one example. Do the first one yourself and get pupils to do others to check that they understand. If demonstrating pairwork you will need a volunteer to help you. Make sure you are near enough to give them a prompt. The overhead projector is very useful for examples, as pupils can see clearly what you are doing and you can also keep eye contact.

Example: Oral work using an exercise in a course book

Don't say: *Bon, maintenant trouvez la page 55. Vous allez travailler avec un partenaire. Vous avez des objets avec des prix, alors une personne doit demander le prix d'un objet et l'autre doit répondre.*

Instead, say:

Trouvez un partenaire. (Indicate possible pairs.)

Trouvez la page 55. (Hold up book to show correct page. Check that they have found it.)

Regardez: 'C'est combien?' (Point out correct section on page.)

Regardez les objets: un manteau, un ... (point to different objects. No need to do all but give examples so they are sure what to look at.)

Un volontaire, s'il vous plaît. (Make sure you are near volunteer.)

Bon. Écoutez! (Regain attention for important part of instructions. Mime listening.)

Whisper to volunteer: *C'est combien un vélo?* (Volunteer repeats.)

Give answer: *Un vélo ... ah oui.* (Make a show of looking for correct object with your finger.)

À vous maintenant. Travaillez avec un partenaire. (You may well need to do more examples before handing over.)

This scenario does not include the introduction or revision of phrases which pupils will need in order to complete the activity in the target language. That issue is dealt with later, but you will need to take account of it in your demonstration.

As understanding grows

As pupils' understanding and confidence increase, the strategies used in the classroom must change to take account of that. In order to continue to improve their language skills, pupils' use and understanding of classroom language must develop in parallel with their general progression. Pupils will also, by this time, have had experience of the kinds of activities you are likely to be doing and this, too, will help them in understanding instructions.

Vary the language

Begin to fill out instructions and vary language, mixing the familiar and the unfamiliar. Key phrases and expressions can now be included in longer sentences and gradually given less individual emphasis, for example: *Écoutez* – will become *Eh bien, maintenant on va écouter une cassette.* Gradually vary vocabulary and expressions. New vocabulary can be conveyed using the same techniques as previously or by using the new word alongside the old one and then dropping the old one, for example: *Silence ... taisez-vous/Silenzio ... tacetevi/Silencio ... cállate.*

Change the support

Begin to withdraw the support offered so that pupils rely more on the actual language for understanding. Gradually reduce the emphasis on mime, gestures, drawings and demonstration and begin to convey meaning through other means such as paraphrasing and giving examples.

Take every opportunity

The more language the pupils hear, the better. Take every opportunity to speak to them either as a whole class or as individuals. Use the beginnings and ends of lessons to talk to individuals about any subject which may interest them. The television, music, sport are all possibilities and there are many more. This will increase their understanding and establish a rapport which will be essential in encouraging them to talk to you.

Written instructions

The same principles apply for written instructions as for oral instructions. From the very beginning give tasks where the written word is supported by pictures, diagrams or examples, just as in oral work meaning is conveyed by actions. An early homework could be to make a badge. This will give pupils confidence in their ability to cope using the support available.

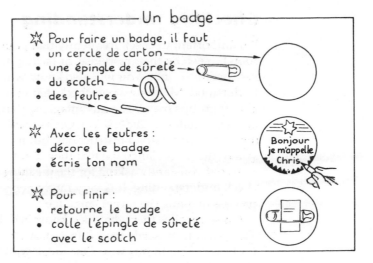

As in oral work, gradually decrease the support so that pupils have to rely more on the language itself. Always give at least one example. Include tasks where pupils have to find the correct part of the instructions for each diagram. In instructions for tasks, use a small set of key words and phrases. Break up the instructions if they are complicated and number them. For example:

1) *Lee las frases.*
2) *Mira los dibujos.*
3) *Escribe la frase apropriada debajo de cada dibujo.*

To begin with, leave out all non-essential language. If there is a title to the activity make sure that it is separate from the instructions. It is useful for pupils to have a glossary of the main terms they are liable to meet in instructions, especially parts of verbs which they are not likely to find in a dictionary.

Using a dictionary

The ability to use a dictionary successfully is a valuable skill to enable pupils to cope in the target language. Introduce it at an early stage for simple activities such as quizzes and crosswords, and encourage pupils to use it frequently. In written instructions it can be helpful to underline important words that it would be helpful for them to look up. As some pupils may wish to buy their own dictionary, it is worth giving advice on the choice of a suitable one. It is obviously helpful if all pupils are using the same.

The use of English

However hard we try, English is not totally avoidable. Many textbooks have instructions, long background passages, or questions written in English, and many tasks require responses given in English (the National Curriculum Orders include the task of interpreting). Make sure, however, that the use of English is unavoidable. There may be a way of changing the task slightly so that it can be done in the target language. For example, the addition of a grid to fill in may make all the difference.

Even if the instructions in the book are in English, you can still use the target language. Background passages can be read in silence or given for homework. Follow-up work as homework or in the next lesson may still be possible in the target language if pupils are given some support, as with a multiple-choice or true/false exercise. Even where answers are required in English, your instructions and reactions can still be given in the target language.

Teacher *Nummer eins, wer weiss diese Antwort? Ja, Peter?*
Pupil (answers in English) She's got a headache.
Teacher *Ja, sehr gut. Sie hat Kopfschmerzen.*

Checking understanding

It is important to check frequently that pupils understand. In most cases this can soon be seen by their response, or lack of it, or by their correct following of instructions or not. You will also know which pupils are likely not to have understood. Make sure you check that they are doing the right thing. Mixed-ability groups may be an advantage, with more able pupils helping their less able classmates to understand. Occasionally it may be necessary to ask pupils if they have understood instructions, but it is far better to teach them how to tell you in the target language that they don't understand.

Avoid constantly asking for the meaning of a word or expression in order to check understanding. It is very rarely necessary and undermines the whole process of using the target language.

It also implies that what they know is only of value if they can translate it. This is not necessarily true. It may, however, be necessary on occasions to check understanding in this way. One quick word in English is better than half a lesson of confusion.

What if they don't understand?

Don't immediately provide pupils with a translation. They will soon realise that this is an easy way out and will not make the effort to listen in future. It also undermines the whole ethos of using the target language. Try explaining in a different way, do another demonstration, get another pupil to interpret, write the key words on the board and get pupils to look them up. Try to make it into a competition to see who can understand you first. If pupils are still at a loss after all this, then change the activity or give a very quick explanation in English. There is no point in wasting a whole lesson especially if it's over one or two words. At the end of the lesson, ask yourself where you went wrong. What didn't you do? What could you have done? Don't despair; these occasions will get fewer and fewer.

Be positive

Remember that our pupils will soon find themselves in situations where they aren't understood when they make the effort to use the target language. If as teachers we get annoyed or give up, we can hardly blame our pupils for doing the same. Show them how to cope with the situation, and treat it with good humour.

Correcting books

In correcting written work we are still addressing the pupil. This, too, should therefore be done in the target language. It is essential, however, that you provide pupils with some means of understanding your comments. If you do not do this, pupils will either not bother to read them, or the giving back of books will be followed by moments of chaos as pupils seek to find out what the comments in their books mean. The same principles apply as before. Try to use a small number of simple phrases which pupils know. A short list to stick in the back of exercise books is helpful, so that pupils have it immediately to hand when they get their books back. If you need to write something different, then emphasise key words by writing them in capitals or underlining them. Encourage pupils to look these words up in a dictionary. Keep a note in your markbook if you have made a complicated comment, so that you can check with the pupil that it has been understood.

What about grammar?

Patterns in structure can be pointed out as successfully in the target language as in English especially if we make them visually obvious. Use different colours to show blocks of words or endings, rub endings out or cover them up. Again, the overhead projector is a valuable aid, as things can be depicted graphically using materials prepared beforehand. Use set phrases to draw pupils' attention to what is important: *Attention/C'est différent/Ça change*. If you wish to use grammatical terms, there is no reason why this cannot be done in the target language. If there is confusion, however, and one or two quick words in English would clear it up, then use them, but make the explanation concise and don't keep switching in and out of the target language. If you do feel a need for a consolidating block of grammar work in English, then keep it clearly separate from the rest of the lesson, and inform pupils when it is happening and when it has finished.

Discipline

Most enforcements of discipline can be carried out effectively in the target language. Indeed, it can be an advantage as it can defuse the situation and turn it into a learning situation. In any case, using the target language will ensure that pupils find it more difficult to argue.

Pupils will not always need to understand what is said. The tone of voice will make it clear that you are angry, and they will know why. As we all know, different tactics work with different pupils at different times. A torrent of reprimand in the target language would silence one pupil but excite another who would respond better to a quick *Un po' di silenzio, per favore!* The same techniques are available to us in the target language as in English, but the addition of another language adds to the possibilities.

In general, try to keep what you say simple and use slow and deliberate gestures to ensure understanding. Punishments can be given in the target language if accompanied by drawings or mime. 'I want to see you after school' can be accompanied by writing the time and room number on the board. If you are giving lines, the appropriate number and content can be written on the board. Sometimes a pupil's need to concentrate on what you are saying is, in itself, an effective means of stopping misbehaviour.

The effectiveness of discipline will, however, be mainly determined by the nature of the class and your relationship with them. If there are major problems, you may, of course, have to resort to English. However, just as you would try to avoid confronting a troublesome pupil in front of the whole class, try to keep the use of English for individuals; or if the whole class needs to be spoken to, keep that separate from the rest of the lesson. If you are looking at your use of the target language, you may well find it more appropriate to begin using it with classes without major discipline problems in order to build up both your confidence and your strategies for discipline.

3 Can pupils use the target language?

If the use of the target language by the teacher is a challenge, an even greater one is that of enabling pupils to use it as well. Pupils cannot be expected to produce language from nowhere, and simple giving them a list of expressions, while helpful in some cases, will not bring total success. In order to ensure this success the necessary language needs to be systematically taught and practised. The language used by pupils can be divided into three categories: 1) activity language 2) reaction language 3) conversational language. These are not distinct or mutually exclusive categories and there are many overlaps, but they form a useful way of approaching the topic.

Activity language

This is the 'survival language' of the classroom – the phrases and expressions which are indispensable if pupils are to function in the classroom, for example: *Je voudrais du papier, Noch einmal, bitte, Non ho capito, He terminado*. Although frequently needed, this type of language cannot be expected to be spontaneously generated, and it is rarely adequately covered in commercial courses. It needs to be consciously and deliberately taught. This involves a lot of planning.

Think ahead

Decide on the basic phrases which pupils will need to use, making them as simple and versatile as possible. How are you going to go about introducing them? When? In what order? Look carefully at what you are teaching. Is there any way you could make it more relevant and immediately useful in the classroom context? This fits in with the demands of communicative methodology, as instead of holding up a ruler and teaching: *Das ist ein Lineal,* you can hold an object behind your back and encourage pupils to ask for things: *Haben Sie ein Lineal, bitte?*

   The demands of communication in the classroom may cause us to re-order what we teach. The alphabet, for example, must be taught at a very early stage if pupils are going to cope with spelling. New structures can be used to improve and develop the language used in the classroom, for example: *Un stylo, s'il vous plaît* can soon become *Je voudrais un stylo/Avez-vous un stylo?/Est-ce que je peux avoir un stylo?* By relating new language learnt to its use in the classroom, pupils can be encouraged to begin to transfer expressions from one context to another.

Plan your activities

In choosing activities give careful thought to the expressions pupils will need in order to complete them successfully in the target language. In the initial lessons in particular, incorporate these expressions into the earlier part of the lesson so that pupils are already familiar with them and can begin to see how they can be re-used in different contexts.

Example: Activity planned for 1st lesson with Year 7 German class

Activity – Pupils work in pairs: pupil 1 writes a number on the back of pupil 2 who has to say the number.
Structure/vocabulary to be practised – *Wieviel ist das?* Numbers 1–10.
Language skills needed to carry out activity:

Pupils decide who starts: *Eins, zwei* (pointing).
Ask if partner is ready: *OK?*
Ask partner to draw number again: *Noch einmal, bitte.*
Tell partner if answer is correct: *Ja/Nein.*
Tell partner that you don't know the answer: (shrug shoulders)

It is evident that simply to introduce all these expressions when demonstrating the activity would leave pupils floundering. If they are to be used effectively by pupils, they should have been included earlier in the lesson, in order to build up to the activity. This is where careful preparation is needed, in introducing the expressions which pupils will need later on. For example:

Eins, zwei – The teacher could use this earlier in the lesson when dividing the class into two teams, or indicating partners in a pair. Pupils could use it if doing short question dialogues in order to decide who starts.

OK? – The teacher could use this earlier if, for example, playing a game in teams where one member of each team has to come and write something on the board. Pupils will soon pick it up as it is so similar to English. At a later stage it will be replaced by a better expression.

Noch einmal, bitte – The teacher can use this expression very early on in class repetition, making pupils repeat each time. Pupils could practise it by doing the same activity in pairs.

(shrug shoulders) – The teacher can use this in demonstrating the activity. It is important that pupils realise from the beginning that they can supplement their linguistic knowledge in communicating by using body language. They must have recourse to the same strategies as the teacher in order to make maximum use of the language at their disposal. Miming is infinitely preferable to the use of English, and is a very useful skill in communication.

Keep it gradual

Try to introduce the classroom phrases gradually. This will mean they are more likely to be remembered and therefore used. The introduction will often be in response to a situation which arises in the classroom, but on other occasions will be planned as part of the lesson. Many expressions can be introduced using simple mime or drawings. Once an expression has been introduced, give pupils plenty of opportunity to practise it. If the situation does not arise naturally, then create it. For example:

Excusez-moi – Tell a pupil to get something from another part of the room but sit or stand in the way and get other pupils to do the same. At the beginning of the lesson stand in the doorway as the class are trying to come in.

Je n'ai pas de – During the lesson go round and take various pens, pencils or books and then give them some written work to do. Alternatively when you give out worksheets, for example, deliberately miss someone out.

Pouvez-vous répéter? – Deliberately say things very quietly or quickly. Encourage pupils to ask when they want a taped listening passage to be repeated. Once they have learnt the phrase, they will not mind asking. Let them decide how many times they need to hear it.

Obviously there will be things which beginners need to say that they cannot say in the target language. Teach them very early on the way to ask how to say things when they need them – *Comment dit-on … en français?*. This will be one of the most valuable things they learn.

Keep revising

As time goes on, the number of phrases known by pupils will increase. However, in order to encourage the continued use of the target language, revise expressions where appropriate. Put a list of useful phrases – *phrases utiles/nützliche Redewendungen/frasi utili/frases utiles* – on the board or the OHP when pupils do an activity so that they can refer to it. Once they get used to the title and what it means, just put the title up and ask them to suggest which expressions would be most useful. Try to introduce one or two new expressions on occasions. When demonstrating the activity, show how these phrases can be used. Take on the role of the less able pupil who might have problems, in order to show how to use the target language, or mime, in these circumstances. Very often, we only show them how to carry out a task with complete success, and it is sometimes when they have problems that they do not have the necessary language or communication strategies. In a board game, for instance, what about the person who cheats, moves the wrong piece, moves the wrong number of squares, has an extra go? Make sure that pupils have the language to cope: *A moi, maintenant/Ich bin dran/Tocca a me/Me toca a mí.* A useful introduction to these phrases can be made by playing games between you and the class. Hold a flashcard the wrong way round and give the class five chances to guess what it is. If they succeed, they get the point; otherwise you do. Once they are used to the game, make mistakes or cheat in the scoring and the class will soon want to know the correct expressions to point this out.

Make it available

However much you practise there will be times when pupils cannot remember the correct phrase. They must know where to find it. Write words and expressions on card and display them round the classroom – on the walls or hanging from the ceiling, or both. Wherever you put them, make sure they are legible. Pupils, too, should have their own personal store of useful classroom language, preferably kept all in one place in a book, so that they know immediately where to look.

Intonation

Demonstrate the value of intonation as well. *Guten Morgen, ich heiße ...* can be conveyed in a number of different ways. Say the same simple phrase or conversation in different moods. Use simple drawings on an OHP transparency to illustrate the moods. Say your basic phrase or dialogue with intonation and expression and encourage pupils to work out which mood you are depicting.

MODESTE　　　　EFFRAYÉ　　　　FURIEUX

Pupils can do the same with a partner. Not only does this show the value of intonation, but it has many other positive benefits. It means that pupils repeat the same phrases several times, thus reinforcing them. It involves pupils' emotions at a very early stage which also reinforces learning. It also provides receptive vocabulary which able pupils will acquire and be able to re-use later.

This kind of activity is particularly important for phrases such as *Oh là là* and *Entschuldigen Sie,* which could be used by pupils in a variety of different situations both in and outside the classroom.

Practice makes perfect

Sometimes, if more time is available, you may wish to practise the classroom language more overtly. Have a stock of small cards for each class showing the expressions they have met. Use these for a variety of activities to make good use of a few spare minutes in a lesson:

- One pupil comes out, is given a card and then has to mime or draw the phrase for the rest of the class to guess. The person who answers correctly does the next one.
- Do the same in groups; the first group to get through a certain number of cards wins.
- Each person in the class is given a card at the beginning of the lesson and then has to try to use the expression at an appropriate point during the lesson.
- If the cards have English on one side and target language on the other, then they can be used in board games where arrival at a certain part of the board means giving the expression on the next card in the pile. For example, a snakes and ladders board can be used where pupils have to answer a question in order to climb a ladder or stay at the top of the snake.

Open-ended activities

More open-ended activities could be included. For example, when television soap operas have scenes set in school, show a brief extract from one of these with the sound turned down and ask pupils to supply the dialogue. This kind of activity can be done at any level. A simple 10-second excerpt showing a pupil putting up his/her hand and a teacher replying is useful at any stage. Pupils can use their imagination especially when they recognise the characters, and at a higher level this can lead to some interesting dialogue (often more interesting than the original). Many comics (*the Beano*, for example) also involve scenes from schools. Blank out the speech bubbles and ask pupils to suggest possibilities. Illustrations from *Le Petit Nicolas* are also good for this. All these involve pupils in more creative use of the target language, thinking through what could possibly be said in a given situation.

© D.C. Thomson & Co. Ltd.

Reaction language

This is the language pupils need to express their reaction to an event or activity – pleasure, disappointment, frustration, commiseration. While this language may not be absolutely essential to the completion of an activity, it adds vitality and atmosphere. Pupils will want to express their reactions and emotions. They must be able to do so in the target language.

Games

To help pupils acquire appropriate expressions, try to include some team games where members from each team compete and the others cheer them on, congratulate them or commiserate with them. A simple example is to draw some items on the board, divide the class into teams and give each person a number. Then simply call out a number and an object, and the appropriate people have to come and rub off the correct object. This can be done at a very early stage and will soon get pupils expressing their feelings. Any team member who uses English will, of course, lose a point. Although this may not make you very popular with teachers in neighbouring classes, it will harness a great deal of enthusiasm and encourage the use of the same phrases later in pair and group activities. Keep phrases very simple especially at the beginning. *Vas-y!, Vite! Bravo!* and *Oh là là!* are all phrases which pupils will enjoy using with great gusto.

Comments

From an early stage, pupils can comment on the difficulty or enjoyment of activities: *Era divertente/interessante/difficile.* When pupils are assessing each other, always encourage them to give a comment as well as a mark. At the beginning you may wish to tell them what comment to give for each mark, for example: 8–10 = *Excellent*, 7–8 = *Très bien.*

Try to use a variety of comments on different occasions. Pupils will soon be able to decide on comments for themselves. At the same time encourage them to comment on tasks and activities, and to react to marks received – *Zut, alors! Chouette! Ça va? Quoi?* With more able pupils this could eventually lead into some discussion of the marks and provide useful feedback as well as giving language practice.

Pupil ownership

Although some of the language for reactions can be predicted, much cannot be. Pupils are unlikely to use the same language in their reactions as we would, and it is important that they are able to say what they themselves want to. Encourage them to ask for translations of the words they would like to use, as they are more likely to use the target language if they can say what they would want to say in English. Often, of course, the translation will not be exact. This will not matter but try to be as accurate as possible. Do not be afraid to say if you don't know an equivalent expression; this will only add to its value for the pupils when you eventually do find it out. A language assistant is invaluable for these phrases. Keep a list on the classroom wall for your assistant to translate on his or her next visit (but give some prior warning), or give a pupil the task of asking the assistant before the next lesson and then reporting back to the class. If you do not have an assistant, then pupils could write to your link school to find out. (The French pupils would probably appreciate learning the English expressions.)

Conversational language

This is the language which pupils may need during the lesson for all those exchanges which are perhaps not vital to the planned activities but which ensure that the lesson runs smoothly, enrich the atmosphere, and contribute to good relationships in the classroom. In lessons in any subject a great deal of the conversation is not directly relevant to the subject of the lesson. Administration and general conversation take a fair amount of time. These conversations can be seen as irrelevant distractions and therefore to be minimised. In language lessons, however, we can turn these exchanges into learning experiences, by carrying them out in the target language, and we should capitalise on this.

Beginning the lesson with greetings

It is very easy to let the beginning and end of each lesson become a meaningless, almost ritualistic exchange. For example:

Teacher *Bonjour, la classe. Ça va?*

Class *Oui, ça va bien, merci.*

This exchange has often been carried out in flat tones by pupils who are either ill or miserable and often totally unaware of what they are saying. If there is to be real communication, pupils (and teacher) must have some choice in their response, with the possibility of the unexpected occurring. Teach a few alternative responses to the initial *Ça va?*/*Wie geht's?*/*Come stai?*/*¿Qué tal?* This can very easily be done with hand actions (thumbs up or thumbs down) or with smiling faces.

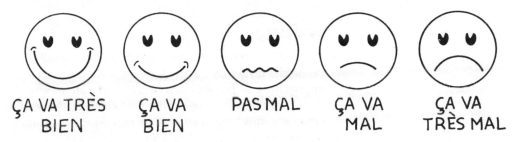

Vary the start, by greeting individual pupils as they arrive and getting them to greet each other and you. Extend this with the suggestion of possible reasons for how they feel, again using mimes or drawings: *Bist du hungrig/durstig/mude?* React to what they say, and teach expressions of shock, horror and surprise. Pupils will gradually begin to use these expressions more actively.

Beginning the lesson in other ways

Another typical start to the lesson is as follows:

Teacher *Buongiorno, ragazzi, che tempo fa?*
Class *Fa caldo.*

This is a good way of revising weather expressions, but it does not involve much real communication as both teacher and class are well aware of what the weather is like. Introduce, instead, expressions for commenting on the weather. *Che afa!* and *Che freddo!* are much more realistic conversation openers. Try beginning by commenting on an event which is known by them all, the type of thing they may talk about themselves, for example: a major news headline (a copy of a newspaper is useful), sports results (local, national or school), the latest events in a soap opera, or the Top Ten. All of these can be tackled at a variety of levels with the pupils' responses ranging from very simple comments *Das ist gut/Das ist nicht gut*, to explaining what exactly has happened.

Ending the lesson

Very often there are a few spare minutes at the end of the lesson and this is an ideal time to resume or continue a conversation between you and the pupils or among the pupils. It is helpful to have a few activities ready for such occasions. A résumé of the lesson is a good idea, especially if pupils are encouraged to express their opinions on the activities. What they are going to do at lunch-time or after school are also possibilities.

Prediction

Particularly popular are 'prediction' activities which can be reported back on during the next lesson: What is the weather going to be like tomorrow? What is for school lunch today? What will a favourite TV character be wearing that night? We obviously need to communicate these to pupils in the target language, so start with a simple one like the Top Ten. Have an OHT ready of last week's Top Ten with the date clearly written on the top, then next to it have a blank list with the date of the next Top Ten on it, and get them to predict where each record will be next week. Pupils will soon get the idea. The record titles will obviously have to be said in English but that would happen abroad anyway. Encourage them to give the titles with a French/German/Italian/Spanish/ Russian accent. (This is in itself a very worthwhile activity highlighting sound differences). Have the OHT available at the beginning of the next lesson to check up on what was said. This kind of activity also has the advantage of giving you a lead-in to your next lesson. The pupils will arrive wanting to talk to you, and report back on what has happened. You will soon be able to extend this to more complicated activities.

Writing

A lot of the above activities could be done equally well as written activities. Using the target language does not always have to mean oral work; it is also important that pupils learn to communicate in writing. For example, get one class to write a message to the next class, or individual pupils could write to the next person who will sit at their seat. These messages might include such things as what kind of mood the teacher is in or how much homework they have.

Use every situation

As language teachers we often spend a lot of time trying to create situations in the classroom where communication will be genuine, and yet often ignore the circumstances which genuinely exist. Reasons for absence or lateness, injuries, lack of uniform and interruptions can all provide the opportunity to introduce and practise new language at a time when it is relevant, rather than later when it may not be. Supply the words and expressions needed as they occur in the classroom situation and give pupils the opportunity to contribute. For example:
– *¿Está Paul?*
– *No, está enfermo/Sí, pero tiene clase de música.*
It is useful to have a selection of OHTs readily available for these predictable occasions.

Interruptions

Interruptions by teachers or other pupils can be turned to your advantage, provided that the visitor is aware of what to do and is sympathetic to your aims. Encourage the class to greet the visitor, and to act as interpreters between the visitor and you. Use the interruption as a talking point when the visitor has left. Another kind of interruption may, of course, come from inside the classroom with the misbehaviour of a pupil. Here the target language can be used to defuse the situation. You could also use it for language practice by involving the class in deciding the punishment, how long to leave the pupil outside, where he or she should sit when allowed to return: *Combien de temps on le/la laisse? Une minute? Deux minutes?* This will of course depend on your relationship with your class and you are the best judge of that.

Individual attention

Take every possible opportunity to have conversations in the target language with individuals in the classroom. If pupils drift in gradually, greet them individually, and talk to individuals as they are getting on with work. Their new hair-do, an injury, the holiday they have just come back from are all possible topics for conversation.

A word of caution

Don't get carried away and ask things which are going to embarrass pupils. It is all too easy, in our enthusiasm for using the target language, to be less sensitive than we would be in English. A pupil will not thank us for having to announce to the whole class that he or she has been to see a social worker or the educational psychologist.

Two-way conversation

Try to avoid 'interrogation' techniques where you are always questioning the pupils. Real communication is always a two-way process. In talking to pupils we should therefore try to share our own ideas, thoughts and experiences as part of the conversation without taking it over. If this two-way relationship is established, pupils will soon want to ask questions. We must make sure that we enable them to do so. Teach pupils to ask questions as well as to answer them and give them opportunities to recall and use these questions. Take advantage of any foreign visitors to the school, and if you have none, invent them. Find a picture of someone in a book or newspaper and copy it onto an OHT. It should be an interesting picture: a famous, intriguing or funny person. Encourage pupils to think how they would begin a conversation with this person. To begin with, suggest possible phrases *Tu as vu …?/Tu as entendu …?* Get them to use these same conversation openers with other members of the class.

Let pupils initiate

If pupils are really going to initiate conversations, they must be aware that this is what we want them to do. It will certainly not be immediately obvious to them. As well as practice, they need opportunity and we must be sufficiently flexible to allow them that. This may seem unrealistic, and it certainly won't be the first priority in the classroom. However, once pupils feel secure in using the target language, there is no reason why they should not begin conversations even at a very simple level, if the pupil-teacher relationship is such that this interaction is encouraged.

Example: Year 10 Italian class (second year of Italian)

Teacher *Buongiorno, ragazzi.*
Class *Buongiorno, Signora, come sta?*
Teacher *Non sto molto bene oggi.*
Class *Perchè?*
Teacher *Ho mal di testa* (miming, as this vocabulary had not yet been met)
Individuals in class *Mamma mia!/Che peccato!/Mi dispiace/Tornare a casa/Silenzio!*
The next day Julie (a pupil in the class) met the teacher in the corridor.
Julie *Buongiorno, Signora. Come sta?*
Teacher *Bene, grazie.*
Julie *E la testa?* (remembering the word from the previous day)
Teacher *Sì, bene.*
Julie *Benissimo.*

This centres around a very simple conversation taken from the beginning of the lesson, but on this occasion the pupils take the initiative and open up the conversation with the question *Come sta?* and then develop it with *Perchè?* Their responses are all taken from responses given by the teacher on various occasions and learnt subconsciously. The most striking thing is the confidence shown by the pupil who the next day initiated the continuation of the conversation. The language is not complicated but she has the confidence, and the desire, to use it to good effect. This confidence comes from practice and a positive experience of using the target language.

4   How do we keep it going?

Having taught and practised the language pupils need to use in the classroom, what can we do to give them the confidence and the desire to continue to use it? Whereas it might seem logical to assume that the use of the target language should get easier as pupils' linguistic experience increases, in reality the opposite is often the case. Pressures of time and course content, and possibly greater discipline problems, combined with adolescent self-consciousness, rebelliousness and peer group pressure, often eat away at good intentions. We must make sure that pupils feel secure in using the target language and confident that their efforts will be met positively.

Be supportive

Just as pupils must make every effort to understand you, afford them equal consideration. When a pupil obviously wants to say something, don't stand back and wait, but offer help and support in finding a means of communicating. The nature of the support given will, of course, vary according to the age and ability of the pupil. It may simply be pointing out where the correct phrase can be found, or it may be guessing what they want to say and thus providing them with the structure and vocabulary, *Tu voudrais un stylo?/Tu voudrais un cahier?* With older or more able pupils, it is often a matter of pointing them towards expressions they have used in different contexts, which they could manipulate. Encourage pupils to use mime, drawing and demonstration. They should have the help of the same communication strategies as you.

Be consistent

The reasoning of 'it would be so much quicker to do it in English' might well seem good on the day, but it often spells the beginning of the end. Try very hard to think of another way round the problem, using all the strategies available to you. Be consistent with your pupils too. Don't let them catch you out by responding to their English without realising, or because it is easier. Show interest and support but claim you don't understand. This is often very hard to do, especially if time is short, but it will be worth it once they get the idea. It may, of course, be that some pupils speak in English in order to waste time or to be deliberately awkward. If you sense that insistence on the target language may cause a major disruption, it may be best to pretend you didn't notice it was said in English, and answer regardless (in the target language, of course).

Be realistic

Remember that the use of the target language is meant to enhance classroom teaching, and not to become an intolerable burden. On the other hand, don't underestimate your pupils: they may well surprise you in what they are capable of. There are, in reality, going to be occasions when pupils will not be able to use the target language. This may be because of the complexity of the message or its urgency. If a pupil informs you that he or she is about to be sick, it would be unwise to delay by insisting on the target language! Try, however, to respond in the target language, unless a delay would lead to catastrophic results. If there is no immediate urgency, help the pupil to say what is needed in the target language. Establish a procedure for those occasions when a pupil needs to say something and is unable to do so in the target language. Teach pupils from the beginning how to ask how to say something: *Wie sagt man ... auf Deutsch?* If there is a need for a longer explanation, a short introductory phrase may be appropriate: *Je dois parler en anglais.* If, of course, you find they have no real need to speak English, then revert to the target language.

It is sometimes useful to have a set period in the lesson when pupils know they can speak to you in English and when problems can be dealt with. Five minutes at the beginning or end or in the middle of the lesson can be helpful, but stick rigidly to this time and let pupils know when it is over. Have a sign in the classroom which you can turn round like an open/closed sign on a shop. Have definite times when the sign allows the use of English, but when it doesn't, make sure this is adhered to. Another similar idea is to have a certain area of the classroom marked, and if you are standing in that area, you and pupils are allowed to use English. It would not be in pupils' interests if they failed to ask questions or discuss problems because of their inability to do so in the target language.

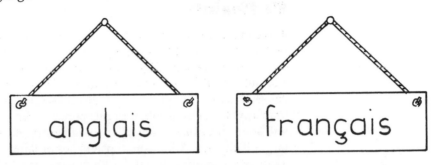

Be non-critical

Greet any attempt in the target language positively or the pupil won't try again. The most important thing is communication, and any understanding of the message (even if only partial) should be rewarded. This is not to say that the correct phrase will not be given, or that more able pupils will not be encouraged to be accurate, but the content should be established and rewarded first. Pupils should be encouraged to be creative in their use of language; this will inevitably lead to errors of which we must be tolerant. Respond first of all to the content of what the pupil has said. If possible, phrase your answer so as to include the correct phrase or give it later, for example:

Pupil *Est-ce que je peux le fenêtre ouvert?*
Teacher *Oui, bien sûr que tu peux ouvrir la fenêtre.*

Be challenging

While asking for the impossible is demotivating, equally demotivating is asking for that which is banal and far below a pupil's capabilities. Our expectations of each individual pupil must be achievable but challenging. Build progression into both your use of the target language and theirs, using, teaching and expecting more complex phrases with older and more able pupils. A year-7 pupil asking for paper would do well to say: *Carta, per favore.* From a pupil in year 12 or 13, *Posso avere un pezzo di carta, per favore?* would be much more appropriate. We can pay lip-service to the target language but completely undervalue it if we fail to build in progression. Encourage pupils to experiment with language and build in new phrases.

Be clear

Don't confuse pupils by responding to the language used rather than the content. This is very easy to say but hard to do. The following conversation took place in an Italian lesson being observed by a student teacher.

Pupil (arriving late) *Mi scusi, Signora, sono andato all'ufficio Signor Taylor.* (He was obviously in trouble).

Teacher *Molto bene* (referring to his correct use of the past tense).

Class *No, molto male! Mamma mia! Perchè?* (referring to his visit to Mr Taylor).

Student teacher (when discussing the incident) – *I would have begun by correcting his rendering of the phrase 'Mr Taylor's office'.*

Of the three responses the teacher's was more positive than the student's would have been but it was nevertheless confusing. It is only the class who actually reacted to what the pupil said, responded appropriately and gave the possibility of developing the conversation. Pupils talk to us in order to communicate a message. If we do not respond to the message, they will be confused by our reaction and may well see no point in communicating. Good use of language must, of course, be acknowledged and rewarded, but pupils must be clear about what is happening.

Be flexible

If we are to encourage the use of the target language we must be sufficiently flexible to respond to what happens in the classroom and to what pupils have to say. In some lessons digression is possible and can bring tremendous advantages. But we all have schemes of work and time-schedules, and there will be other lessons when we can't afford to deviate from our plans. More effective than anything else is when pupils perceive the target language as effective. They will soon learn that requests are much more likely to be granted if made in the target language. Allow small privileges or leniencies from time to time if pupils have made an effort to ask for them in the target language. The momentary inconvenience of allowing them to do something like listening to music while they work will be more than compensated for by their motivation to use the target language.

Make it worthwhile

One possible obstacle to the extensive use of the target language by the pupils in the classroom could be a lack of perceived reward or acknowledgement of their efforts. It has in the past not been 'marked' in the same sense as most other more formal tasks. With the advent of the National Curriculum this will, of course, have to change and we will become familiar with methods of assessing and recording what takes place in the classroom. This is essential if we are really to reward pupils' achievements.

Be aware of what pupils are doing in the classroom. Make a special effort to listen to two or three pupils each lesson or each week and make a note of how they are performing. Keep these notes in one place, for example in an exercise book kept in your desk, and make sure they are dated. You can then transfer them to individual records when you have time. Make a note, too, of anything exceptional said by a pupil which shows a development in their use of the target language. We should be able to see progress in terms of pupils' increased confidence and willingness to express themselves as well as in the complexity of language used. Give marks and/or feedback on this, make a space for it on the Record of Achievement, and discuss individual progress with them.

Don't go to extremes

The use of the target language in the classroom is meant to simulate the conditions and atmosphere which would be met on a visit abroad. Nothing would destroy this more than the teacher rushing to tick boxes and make a note of every remark made by the pupil. We could end up being so busy recording the use of the target language that we don't have time to encourage it. We cannot hope to note everything every single pupil says or does, and should not attempt it. In the end, assessment is a matter of our awareness and professional judgement of what is happening in the classroom.

Use the pupils

It is most important that pupils understand what we are looking for in assessing them. They can often be unaware of how much English they are speaking or how much target language. As well as receiving our feedback, pupils should have the opportunity to assess themselves and each other. Try giving everyone in the class someone else to observe for a week or two and then feed back their impressions. Instead of putting pupils into twos for pairwork, have groups of three with one person observing and reporting back. The same could happen in group activities. Pupils could be encouraged to assess each other both in terms of their ability to say and do certain specific things, and in terms of their overall general ability and confidence. A sample record sheet for duplication can be found on page 29.

Involving the pupils

If you want other, more graphic means of recording effort and progress in using the target language, especially when you begin, consult your class for ideas. They are more likely to be motivated if they have been involved. There are many possibilities, such as stars stuck on a chart or smiling faces in their exercise books, and pupils are bound to think of many others. One class decided they would pay a fine every time they spoke English unnecessarily in the classroom, putting the money towards a party at the end of the year. Beware – the teacher has to pay fines too! If you try to capture their imagination, you are halfway there.

Promote a positive attitude

The most important thing is that pupils should not feel threatened and it is up to us to make sure that they don't. We must present the use of the target language not as something we are imposing on them but as something we are going to do with them, and in which all have a part to play. Discuss possible difficulties with them, and how these can be coped with. Share targets and success criteria with them, and let them know when these are being achieved. Above all, we can promote a positive and enthusiastic attitude by being positive ourselves.

5 What do I need to think about?

A departmental policy

To ensure consistency, it is essential to have a policy on the use of the target language in the classroom which everyone agrees to and is working towards. This policy should contain the rationale for the use of the target language, as well as how it is to be implemented and evaluated. The use of the target language will be most effective where it is consistent throughout the department. Pupils must know what to expect as they move from one teacher to another, and one class to another. Teachers must know that all pupils have had the same experience. No one person must be cast in the role of that 'strange teacher who never speaks English'. Many points need to be considered, however.

Associated questions

Any change in practice will inevitably affect other things that go on within a school. There are a number of questions which need to be thought about, such as:
- How are languages staff going to talk to each other when pupils are listening?
- How are you going to speak to pupils outside the classroom? In the languages area? In the rest of the school?
- How are you going to speak to other members of staff who come into your lessons? How will you expect them to respond?
- How does your policy on the use of the target language affect your policy on marking books, and presentation of books by pupils?

Information giving

Is there anybody else in the school who should be informed of any of the decisions in your policy, for example senior management, in-class support teachers? Maybe the rest of the staff ought to be aware of your policy and know what to expect if they come into your lessons for any reason. If they understand they will be more in sympathy; otherwise they may just feel you are trying to embarrass them. Explain to them, too, how they could help you in your aims. It is, of course, important for pupils to see other people using the target language to communicate; it is particularly useful if people who are not language teachers can be seen to have effective language skills.

Implementation and success criteria

The mark of an effective policy is a clear understanding of how to go about bringing it into practice. Decide on your first steps and make them manageable. It is better to start in a modest way, to succeed and be motivated to go further than to try to do too much and fail dismally. You may aim to start with one particular year group, or with the class you find easiest, or you may aim to develop your skills in one area first, for example giving instructions. Whatever you decide to do, go for it. Don't be tempted to put it off. You will always find excuses if you look for them.

Pupil involvement

How are you going to share what you are doing with the pupils? This is very important especially if you are beginning to use the target language with older groups who are not used to it. If they are going to be involved and cooperate, they need to know why you are doing it, what part they have to play, and how it will benefit them. Make sure they know exactly what they should be aiming at; break it into manageable steps for them as well. They could have some input into how to tackle it, devising a reward/record system, or providing some artwork if you need it to explain pupils' phrases. Discuss potential problems with them and how these should be tackled. Once you have done this, be prepared to start immediately. If you leave it, you will lose their initial enthusiasm.

Language

You will need to decide on the main words and expressions you are going to use (see pages 30–60). These will fall into several categories:

    Teachers' spoken instructions

    Phrases for pupil use

    Comments to be made in exercise books

    Written instructions to be used on worksheets.

    Many of these phrases may well be decided by the type of instructions given in the course you use. Many of the courses available give instructions in the target language, and you will want to build on the language used there, rather than introducing different expressions.

Resources

If your coursebook uses a lot of English, you may find it in conflict with your new policy. Given that you may not be able to afford a new course, how are you going to tackle this? You may be able to improve the situation in a variety of ways by producing some extra resources to go with it. Maybe the next time you get worksheets reprinted, you could blank out the English instructions and put them in the target language. Whatever you decide to do, a lot of time and energy would be saved by working on it as a department, and the pooling of resources will aid the successful implementation of the policy throughout the department.

Schemes of work

The language introduced for use in the classroom is an integral part of what you do and therefore needs to be included in the Scheme of work. As regards the phrases for pupil use in particular, you will want to decide in what approximate order and at what time they are going to be introduced. This will not be stuck to rigidly, as it will partly depend on need. It is, however, important that a teacher taking over somebody else's class knows what they have done, and that pupils who change groups do not suddenly find themselves completely lost. Is there anything in the Scheme of work which needs to be changed in order to facilitate the use of the target language in the classroom? Is there anything which could be related to a classroom context in order to improve pupils' use of the language? Is there any progression in the language you will expect them to use in the classroom? How is the use of the language in the classroom going to be assessed?

Reference

Pupils must know where to look in order to find the expressions they need, both in the classroom and in their books. This again should be decided as a department. In the classroom phrases can be displayed on walls, ceilings or both, although some phrases such as *Excusez-moi d'être en retard* may be better placed outside the classroom. What are teachers who teach more than one language going to do? One solution is to put different languages in different colours. If you are going to use signs, symbols and drawings to convey what these phrases on the walls mean, will these be uniform throughout the department? Pupils could, of course, be used to design them for you. Try to establish one place to keep classroom phrases – the back or middle of a vocabulary book, for example – so that pupils will always know where to find them.

Display

One of the aims of using the target language is to try to create the conditions the pupils would meet if they were abroad. Also important in this is the general ambience in the department and in the classrooms. When pupils enter the classroom, does the display around them reinforce the idea that they are in a different country and must speak a different language? Good displays can help greatly in increasing exposure to the target language, and making vocabulary available. There should be a lot of language around for pupils to see and read, as well as posters and pictures. Put up signs in the languages taught. Even signs such as 'Fire Exit' can have translations underneath them.

Support

Within the department you will, hopefully, be supporting each other on an informal basis by sharing how things are going. It may be helpful to do other things as well, such as sharing lesson preparation, or even observing each other. Don't forget the needs of the non-specialist teacher. Do some INSET activities within the department, practising giving instructions through mime or in the target language. The opportunity to observe others is also a useful means of support for the non-specialist and specialist alike. Even if you are all specialist teachers, some of you may be teaching a language in which you are not very confident. Assistants, too, will be in need of guidance and support. Help them to simplify their use of language, and let them know what instructions and phrases pupils are used to. What may seem obvious to us will not be to the assistants. When they are observing lessons when they first arrive, get them to note in particular how the target language is used.

Review

If you are working as a team, it is very important that a date is set for reviewing what is happening. This will make sure that everybody does as has been agreed without putting it off, and it will also make sure that the review happens. As with any change or innovation, review is essential in order to evaluate and improve. Teachers will need the opportunity to share concerns and discuss possible answers to these concerns. Common concerns could give rise to INSET activities. However, it is equally important to share successes, as it is success that will build the confidence and motivation to continue. Strategies which have worked well can also be raised and discussed.

The discussion of achievements and progress may lead to the setting of new targets. You may well decide to extend what you are doing to other classes or to try out new strategies in order to implement your policy more fully. This will in turn result in a new review date.

6 But how can I cope if...?

How can I cope...

... if I'm teaching a language I don't feel confident in?

In some ways you are at an advantage as you should find it relatively easy to keep your language simple. You will also feel a great deal of empathy with the pupils and their efforts to communicate in the target language. The support of other teachers is invaluable here, in providing you with key phrases and expressions. The best help of all is to attend a few lessons given by a specialist teacher to glean the most useful ones. Don't try to learn them all at once; you will never remember them. Prepare your lessons thoroughly and prepare your instructions. Ask colleagues for help in working out what you should say, and then use it as often as possible so that it becomes second nature. Note down all these expressions and keep them in one place for easy reference. Try to add some new expressions to your repertoire every week.

If you get stuck in the middle of a lesson, try to communicate your message by some other means, such as mime or demonstration. If you get stuck in the middle of a sentence, do your best or make it up! No pupil is going to remember something you say fleetingly in passing (especially since as a non-specialist you are unlikely to be teaching advanced groups). It is far more important that your pupils get used to coping with the target language than that absolutely everything they hear is perfectly correct. A word of caution, however: make a note to find out for next time what you should have said. If you keep on saying something incorrectly, not only will your pupils begin to think it's correct but so will you.

... if the pupils don't want to know?

Hopefully, if you do everything you can to involve them in your preparations, this situation won't arise, but sometimes it does. Set short-term targets: try to do ten minutes in the target language and shower them with praise when they manage it. Next lesson try to make it longer. If you are doing part of the lesson in the target language, make it the most enjoyable part in terms of activities – a bit of elementary psychology should get them to associate target language with fun activities. Make the effort to encourage individuals: when no-one else is listening tell them how well they did in the target language session. You should soon get at least a few defectors to your side, and then you will be well on the path to success.

... if the rest of the department don't use the target language?

This is certainly not an ideal situation, as not only will you be working alone, but you will also be taking over classes who aren't used to using the target language, and having to re-establish a pattern of working. Do not despair, however. Perhaps there is someone in a nearby school with whom you can share ideas, successes and failures? In any case, pupils have a remarkable ability to adapt to the requirements and expectations of different teachers. Take time to explain to new classes how you work and why. Give a list of useful phrases to older students and give them practice in using them. Meanwhile, make sure other staff hear about what is going on in your classroom. Nothing will convince them more than success.

…if pupils speak to each other in English as soon as my back is turned?

It is inevitable that this will happen to a certain extent. (If we go abroad with English-speaking people, we usually speak to each other in English unless there is someone else present.) In some circumstances we may want it to happen: if one pupil is interpreting for another, for example, or helping another pupil to work out what to say. Distinguish between this type of conversation and the exchanges which are part of pairwork and groupwork. Explain to pupils that they have not successfully completed the activity unless they have done so in the target language. If they are assessing themselves and each other, then they will have to continue in the target language even when you are not watching.

…if pupils in my class are low attainers?

There are several advantages with a low-ability class. There is generally less pressure of time in terms of course content, so that you can afford to spend more time on the target language used in the classroom. The needs are generally very repetitive (for example, there is generally someone who has not got a pen). The target language is also particularly motivating for this kind of pupil. Long-term aims, such as the possibility of going abroad some day or even an exam in a few years' time, are irrelevant for them. They need to see the short-term relevance of what they are doing, and using the target language in the classroom is one way of providing this relevance.

Concentrate on a few basic and adaptable phrases which can be used in a variety of situations. Encourage the pupils to use every means available to them in order to communicate: mime, drawing, demonstration, etc. In reality, if these pupils were to go abroad, they would not have a great deal of language at their disposal. By using the target language in the classroom, we are giving them essential practice in using the small amount of language they do have to maximum effect. Encourage them to function as a group, helping each other to communicate. Make a class activity or challenge out of trying to get the message across.

Example: Year 11 French low-ability class (with a large disruptive element)

The class were doing a listening task from a cassette. The teacher gave instructions in the target language and then played the cassette.

Class *Répétez, s'il vous plaît, madame.*

Teacher *Oui* (played again).

The class still found it difficult as it was quite long. They wanted the cassette paused, and there followed some discussion amongst pupils about how they were going to convey this to the teacher. They eventually came up with three alternatives and decided to try them all:

1. *Ré … pé … tez* (said very slowly)
2. *Pausez la cassette.*
3. *Répétez. STOP. Répétez. STOP. Répétez. STOP.*

All three of these were accompanied by appropriate mimes of pressing the pause button on the cassette. The class talked in English together but their discussion was very productive, both in terms of the thought processes they went through as a group and the final result. Because it was a group challenge, they did not feel threatened by it, and even the most disruptive element became involved in the task.

... if I don't feel confident?

Take heart! Most people don't feel confident when they start to try something out. Confidence comes when you begin to see success, and then it grows. Don't try to do everything at once but give yourself manageable steps to take. Start with the class you feel most confident with. Take careful note of your successes, those moments when you see a reward for your efforts and when communication really happens in your classroom. Build on those successes and share them with others, too. The encouragement will be mutual.

7 Is it all possible?

The use of the target language

The use of the target language, then, is not in itself difficult. The difficult thing is starting to use it. There are many things to think about, as when you learn to drive a car, but gradually these become automatic and the process becomes second nature.

Teacher's and pupils' use of the language and the teacher's responses will all fit together in the classroom situation. We should then see pupils growing in confidence and being more willing to express themselves, using the language they have at their disposal to maximum effect. The greatest encouragement comes from success, no matter how limited, and using the target language enables success to come from every situation, even those which in other circumstances might be a disturbance or a distraction.

Example: Conversation in a low-ability year-8 class

Ben (a low attainer) is, yet again, leaning back on two legs of his chair.

Teacher *Ben, dein Stuhl!*

Ben *Entschuldigen Sie.* (He sits properly for five minutes and then swings back again.)

Teacher *Ben, dein Stuhl! Steh auf!* (giving hand action for 'stand up')

Ben (pleadingly) *Nein, entschuldigen Sie.*

Teacher *Ben!*

Ben (grudgingly) *Ja.* (Ben stands up for five minutes until teacher sets some written work.)

Ben *Entschuldigen Sie, kann ich bitte … ?* (He mimes sitting down.)

Teacher *Ja, setz dich.*

Ben *Danke schön.*

A few minutes later the teacher is sitting with a group of pupils and leans back on her chair to help a pupil behind her.

Ben (triumphantly) *Entschuldigen Sie, dein Stuhl!*

Teacher (goes on sitting) *Entschuldigung.*

Ben *Nein* (giving hand action for 'stand up').

Teacher *Steh auf?*

Ben *Ja.*

The teacher stands up for the rest of the lesson.

The teacher's use of language

In this conversation neither Ben nor the teacher uses a great deal of language, and yet they manage to communicate perfectly. There is no need for Ben to be told what is wrong with his chair: he is well aware and has been told off about it many times before. The teacher does not point to the chair; this has been done on previous occasions, but Ben has now heard it so many times he needs no support in understanding. The phrase *Steh auf* is accompanied by a hand action in order to ensure comprehension. This is the first time that this punishment has been used.

The pupil's use of language

Ben manages to communicate a great deal using very few words. He uses the phrase *Entschuldigen Sie* in four different contexts with four different intonations and to great effect. Ben knows the phrase *Kann ich bitte … ?* because he is someone who quite often forgets his pen and has to borrow one, but he is able to transfer it to a new context. The word he doesn't know he mimes in order to make himself understood. *Dein Stuhl* he was able to produce because he has heard it often and learnt it subconsciously and again he supplies the unknown phrase by mime and not by resorting to English. Ben has the confidence to initiate an exchange by imitating what he has heard the teacher do on previous occasions.

The teacher's response

The teacher responds throughout to the message Ben is communicating. In both cases where he mimes, that is understood and responded to but the phrase is supplied in the teacher's response. Where *du* and *Sie* are mixed up, this is rightly ignored. Most importantly, the teacher finishes the lesson standing up; this is Ben's reward for his efforts and an observer could see that he was well pleased with himself. The teacher did, in fact, congratulate him on his use of the language later on, but not in the course of the conversation where the most important thing was to respond to what he said.

This is the kind of situation which occurs in hundreds of classrooms every day. The use of the target language can turn every occurrence into a learning situation, and demonstrate the practical use of what is being taught. Using the target language is not an end in itself but a means to an end. That end is to enhance the learning process for our pupils and to give them the confidence they need in order to make effective use of the language they acquire.

Producing a policy on the use of the target language

Discussion documents

Modern Foreign Languages National Curriculum Final Report DES October 1990

'The natural use of the target language for virtually all communication is a sure sign of a good modern language course. Learners are enabled to see that the language is not only an object of study but also an effective medium for conducting the normal business of the classroom … Skilfully used and combined with judicious checking of pupil understanding, this kind of language input contributes to learners' knowledge and skills and to their awareness of language as both instrument and human link. It is important that every modern languages department establishes a clear policy for the use of the target language in the classroom.' para 10.7.

'Communicating in a foreign language must thus involve both teachers and pupils using the target language as the normal means of communication.' para 3.18.

Modern Foreign Languages Non-statutory Guidance NCC February 1992

'Departments should agree on a policy for consolidating or extending the use of the target language by teachers and pupils, to ensure that the target language is used consistently by all members of the department with shared expectations of pupils' use of it.' para 1.7.

Questions to address

- **Rationale** – Why is the use of the target language in the classroom desirable?
- **Method** – How is this language going to be introduced and practised? What opportunities will be provided for pupils and what support will be given?
- **Development** – How will progression and differentiation be assured?
- **Assessment** – How will the pupils' use of the target language be assessed and recorded?
- **Evaluation** – How will the department evaluate the implementation of the policy? What are the success criteria?
- **Implications** – What are the implications of the policy for other policies, resources, the classroom environment, other people?

Checklist

- Is there a departmental policy? Do I agree with it?
- What are my immediate aims? Where am I going to start? What am I going to develop?
- How am I going to involve my pupils?
- Have I decided on key words and expressions?
- How am I going to introduce these?
- Have I displayed these expressions in the classroom, or made a space for them to be displayed?
- Is there anything else I can display in my classroom to encourage the use of the target language?
- Where are pupils going to write down useful expressions?
- What am I going to do if I get stuck?
- Do my pupils know what to do if they get stuck?
- Is there anywhere where my coursebook conflicts with my aims? If so, how am I going to cope with that?
- Do I need to change any of the resources I use?
- How am I going to evaluate success? How am I going to communicate success to my pupils?
- How and when am I going to review what I am doing?

Pupil record sheet – Use of language

Name .... Language ....

In the classroom

I can understand when the teacher asks me to:
- ☐ repeat something
- ☐ put up my hand
- ☐ listen
- ☐ find a partner
- ☐ get out my book

I can understand when the teacher asks:
- ☐ if I am ready
- ☐ if I have finished
- ☐ if I have understood

I can say when:
- ☐ I don't understand
- ☐ I don't know the answer
- ☐ I don't know how to say or spell something
- ☐ I want something repeated

I am able to:
- ☐ say if I like something
- ☐ say if I don't like something
- ☐ say if I am pleased
- ☐ congratulate someone
- ☐ attract the teacher's attention

I have used the language to:
- ☐ work with a partner
- ☐ work in a group
- ☐ play a game
- ☐ work on the computer

☐ I listen hard and try to understand what is said.

☐ I can understand the words for most of the things in the classroom.

☐ I understand short simple instructions.

☐ There are lots of words and phrases the teacher uses which I understand.

☐ I usually manage to understand what the teacher says even though I don't know every word.

☐ I have no real problems understanding what the teacher says even though I don't know every word.

☐ I know the words for some classroom objects.

☐ I know a few simple phrases and I use them whenever possible.

☐ I can use a lot of short simple phrases.

☐ If I don't know how to say something, I can find it out.

☐ I can usually manage to make myself understood, even if I don't know the correct expressions.

☐ I can change the expressions I have learnt in order to say something different.

☐ I can use a lot of phrases without having to think about it.

☐ I can usually work out how to say what I want to.

Language for classroom use: French

Language for teacher use

General classroom requests and instructions

Sit down	**Assieds-toi/Asseyez-vous**
Stand up	**Lève-toi/Levez-vous**
Switch the light on/off	**Allume/Éteins**
Put up your hand	**Lève/Levez la main**
Quiet, please	**Silence, s'il te/vous plaît**
Have you finished?	**As-tu fini?/Avez-vous fini?**
Where is your ...?	**Où est ton/ta ...?**
Get out your ...	**Sors ton/ta/tes .../Sortez votre/vos ...**
Please repeat	**Répète, s'il te plaît/Répétez, s'il vous plaît**
All together	**Tous ensemble**
A volunteer, please	**Un(e) volontaire, s'il vous plaît**
Come here	**Viens/Venez ici**
Do you understand?	**Tu comprends?/Vous comprenez?**
Speak a bit louder	**Parle/Parlez un peu plus fort**
Speak more quietly, please	**Parle/Parlez moins fort**
Say it in ..., please	**Dis-le en ..., s'il te plaît/Dites-le en ..., s'il vous plaît**
Who would like to read?	**Qui veut lire?**
Try again	**Essaie-le/Essayez-le encore**
Give out the books	**Distribue/Distribuez les livres**
Collect the books	**Ramasse/Ramassez les livres**
Write down your homework	**Écris/Écrivez ce qu'il faut faire comme devoirs**
Give in your homework	**Rends tes devoirs/Rendez vos devoirs**
Learn for a test	**Apprends/Apprenez pour une interro orale**
Please open the window	**Ouvre la fenêtre, s'il te plaît**
Please close the window	**Ferme la fenêtre, s'il te plaît**
Who got it right?	**Qui a juste?**
Put your things away	**Rangez vos affaires**
Stand behind your chairs	**Mettez-vous derrière vos chaises**
Put up your chairs	**Mettez vos chaises sur les tables**
Stack your chairs	**Empilez vos chaises**
Put your bags on the floor	**Mettez vos sacs par terre**
Sit in a circle	**Mettez-vous en cercle**

Expressions of praise

Quite good	**Assez bien**
Well done!	**Bravo!**
Very good	**Très bien**
Excellent	**Excellent**
Good try	**Bon effort**
Congratulations!	**Félicitations!**
Not bad	**Pas mal**
Much better	**Beaucoup mieux**
OK	**Passable**
Wonderful!	**Merveilleux!**
Brilliant!	**Super!**
Good idea	**Bonne idée**
Original	**Original**

Expressions of reprimand/criticism

Line up quietly	**En rang et en silence**
Take off your coat(s)	**Enlève le manteau/Enlevez les manteaux**
Be quiet	**Tais-toi/Taisez-vous**
There is too much noise	**Il y a trop de bruit**
That's enough	**Ça suffit**
Don't shout out	**Ne crie pas/Ne criez pas les réponses**

Pay attention	**Concentre-toi/Concentrez-vous**
Calm down	**Calme-toi/Calmez-vous**
Don't be silly	**Ne sois pas stupide/Ne soyez pas stupides**
Are you chewing?	**Tu manges/Vous mangez quelque chose?**
Put it in the bin	**Mets-le/Mettez-le à la poubelle**
You can do better	**Tu peux/Vous pouvez faire mieux**
Turn round	**Tourne-toi/Tournez-vous**
Don't swing back on your chair	**Ne te balance pas sur ta chaise**
Sit properly	**Assieds-toi/Asseyez-vous bien**
Come back after school	**Reviens après les cours**
Lines	**Lignes à copier**
Detention on (day) at (time)	**Colle le (jour) à (heure)**
Look this way	**Regarde/Regardez par ici**

Instructions for activities

Find a partner	**Trouve/Trouvez un(e) partenaire**
Get into groups of ...	**Formez des groupes de ...**
Find page ...	**Trouve/Trouvez la page ...**
Copy this into your books	**Copiez ça dans vos cahiers**
In the back of your books	**Au dos de votre cahier**
In the front of your books	**À l'avant de votre cahier**
Write in the margin	**Écris/Écrivez-le au brouillon**
Leave a line	**Saute/Sautez une ligne**
Swap books	**Échange ton cahier/Échangez vos cahiers**
Fill in the grid	**Remplis/Remplissez le tableau**
Correct your work	**Corrige ton travail/Corrigez votre travail**
Mark each other's work	**Corrigez le travail de votre voisin(e)**
Read this	**Lis/Lisez ça**
Draw and label	**Dessine/Dessinez et écris/écrivez le nom dessous**
Draw a picture	**Dessine/Dessinez une image**
Ask questions	**Pose/Posez des questions**
Answer the questions	**Réponds/Répondez aux questions**
Ask your partner	**Demande à ton/ta partenaire/Demandez à votre partenaire**
Don't let your partner see	**Ne laisse pas ton/ta partenaire voir/Ne laissez pas votre partenaire voir**
Cover this with your hand	**Couvre ça avec ta main/Couvrez ça avec votre main**
Tick the boxes	**Coche/Cochez les cases**
Copy the grid	**Copie/Copiez la grille**
Fill in the gaps	**Remplis/Remplissez les blancs**
Join up the words and pictures	**Relie/Reliez les mots aux images**
Mix up the cards	**Mélange/Mélangez les cartes**
Look it up in the dictionary	**Cherche-le/Cherchez-le dans le dictionnaire**
Pretend that you are ...	**Imagine que tu es/Imaginez que vous êtes ...**
Mime	**Mime/Mimez**
Do the role-play	**Jouez le jeu de rôle**
Have a conversation	**Conversez**
Take it in turns	**Faites-le à tour de role**
Imagine	**Imagine/Imaginez**
Think of ...	**Pense/Pensez à ...**
Whisper	**Murmure/Murmurez**
Team A, B, C	**Équipe A, B, C**
Stand in line	**Mettez-vous en ligne**
You have five minutes	**Tu as/Vous avez cinq minutes**
Start with ...	**Commence/Commencez par**
Rewind the cassette	**Rembobine/Rembobinez la cassette**
Listen to the cassette	**Écoute/Écoutez la cassette**
Record on cassette	**Enregistre/Enregistrez sur cassette**
Record on video	**Enregistre/Enregistrez sur vidéo**
Put the disk in the disc drive	**Introduis/Introduisez la disquette**
Load the programme	**Charge/Chargez le programme**
Type in ...	**Tape/tapez**
Delete	**Efface/Effacez**

Press	**Appuie/Appuyez**
Save	**Sauvegarde/Sauvegardez**
Print your work	**Imprime ton travail/Imprimez votre travail**

Explanations (grammar)

Look at this	**Regarde/Regardez ceci**
Notice this	**Remarque/Remarquez ça**
It's different	**C'est différent**
It changes	**Ça change**
It's important	**C'est important**
Take away this	**Enlève/Enlevez ceci**
Put	**Mets/Mettez**
Don't forget	**N'oublie pas/N'oubliez pas**
It's masculine	**C'est masculin**
It's feminine	**C'est féminin**
It's neuter	**C'est neutre**
It begins with …	**Cela commence par …**
It ends with …	**Cela finit en …**
An ending	**Une terminaison**

Comments in exercise books

Good work	**Bon travail**
Neat work	**Bien présenté**
Take more care	**Fais plus attention**
Too many mistakes	**Trop de fautes**
Too short	**Trop court**
Take more care with spelling	**Attention à l'orthographe**
Take more care with your handwriting	**Attention à ton écriture**
You can do better	**Tu peux faire mieux**
Good presentation	**Bonne présentation**
Where is your homework?	**Où sont tes devoirs?**
See me!	**Viens me voir!**
Underline the title	**Souligne le titre**
Don't forget the date and title	**N'oublie pas la date et le titre**
Don't leave gaps	**Ne laisse pas d'espaces**
A big improvement	**Une bonne amélioration**
Write in sentences	**Écris en formant des phrases**
Don't write in English	**N'écris pas en anglais**
Copy with more care	**Copie avec plus d'attention**

Phrases for pupil use

To the teacher

Can you repeat that?	**Pouvez-vous répéter ça?**
Can you repeat that more slowly?	**Pouvez-vous répétez ça plus lentement?**
How do you say … in …?	**Comment dit-on … en …?**
What does … mean?	**Qu'est-ce que … veut dire?**
How do you spell …?	**Comment ça s'écrit, …?**
I've/I haven't finished	**J'ai/Je n'ai pas fini**
I don't understand	**Je ne comprends pas**
I don't know	**Je ne sais pas**
Is that right?	**C'est juste?**
Excuse me	**Excusez-moi**
Sorry	**Désolé(e)**
Just a minute	**Un moment**
I haven't got a …	**Je n'ai pas de …**
I've forgotten my pen	**J'ai oublié mon stylo**
I've forgotten my homework	**J'ai oublié mes devoirs**
May I have a piece of paper?	**Est-ce que je peux avoir du papier?**
What page is it?	**C'est quelle page?**

Sorry I'm late	**Désolé(e), je suis en retard**
May I go to the toilet?	**Est-ce que je peux aller aux toilettes?**
May I leave?	**Est-ce que je peux sortir?**
May I go to my violin lesson?	**Est-ce que je peux aller à mon cours de violon?**
I feel ill	**Je ne me sens pas très bien**
Can you help me?	**Pouvez-vous m'aider?**
I have a problem	**J'ai un problème**
I didn't hear	**Je n'ai pas entendu**
I can't see	**Je ne vois pas bien**
May I open the window?	**Est-ce que je peux ouvrir la fenêtre?**
May I close the window?	**Est-ce que je peux fermer la fenêtre?**
… is away	**… est absent(e)**
I was away	**J'étais absent(e)**
Can you explain …?	**Pouvez-vous expliquer …?**
May I clean the board?	**Est-ce que je peux effacer le tableau?**

Classroom objects

Book	**Le livre**
Exercise book	**Le cahier**
Pen	**Le stylo**
Biro	**Le Bic**
Pencil	**Le crayon**
Rubber	**La gomme**
Ruler	**La règle**
Scissors	**Les ciseaux**
Glue	**La colle**
Sellotape	**Le scotch**
Rough/scrap paper	**Le papier de brouillon**
Compass	**Le compas**
Hole punch	**La perforatrice**
Highlighter	**Le surligneur**
Stapler	**L'agrafeuse (f)**
Drawing pin	**La punaise**
Paper clip	**Le trombone**
Calculator	**La calculatrice**
Felt-tip pen	**Le feutre**
Pencil case	**La trousse**
Dictionary	**Le dictionnaire**
School bag	**Le cartable/Le sac**
Cassette	**La cassette**
Tape recorder	**Le magnétophone**
Listening centre	**Le centre à écouteurs**
Headphones	**Le casque à écouteurs**
Video	**La vidéo**
Video player	**Le magnétoscope**
Video camera	**La caméra**
Television	**La télé(vision)**
Computer	**L'ordinateur (m)**
Keyboard	**Le clavier**
Screen	**L'écran (m)**
Disc	**La disquette**
Disc drive	**Le lecteur de disquette**
Printer	**L'imprimante (f)**
Concept keyboard	**Le clavier tactile**
Concept keyboard overlay	**La feuille témoin**
Blackboard	**Le tableau noir**
Chalk	**La craie**
Board rubber	**La brosse du tableau**
Whiteboard	**Le tableau blanc**
Whiteboard pen	**Le feutre pour tableau blanc**
Overhead projector	**Le rétroprojecteur**
Overhead transparency	**Le transparent**
Projector	**Le projecteur**

Games

Dice	**Les dés (m)**
Counter	**Le pion**
Cards	**Les cartes**
Board	**Le plateau de jeux**
Shake the dice	**Remue/Remuez les dés**
Throw the dice	**Lance/Lancez les dés**
Go forward to …	**Avance/Avancez jusqu'à la case …**
Go back to …	**Retourne/Retournez à la case …**
Go back to the start	**Retourne/Retournez à la case départ**
Have another throw	**Relance/Relancez les dés**
Odd/Even number	**Le nombre impair/pair**
The winner	**Le gagnant/La gagnante**
Guess	**Devine/Devinez**
Miss a turn	**Passe ton tour/Passez votre tour**
Turn over	**Retourne/Retournez**
Deal out the cards	**Distribue/Distribuez les cartes**
Pick up a card	**Prends/Prenez une carte**
Collect pairs	**Collectionne/Collectionnez les paires**
Collect sets of …	**Collectionne/Collectionnez la série des …**

Talking to each other

I'll start	**Je commence**
You can start	**Tu commences**
I'm person A	**Je suis A**
You're person B	**Tu es B**
Whose turn is it?	**C'est à qui le tour?**
It's your turn	**C'est ton tour**
It's my turn	**C'est mon tour**
What?	**Comment?**
Can you repeat that	**Tu peux répéter ça?**
Who's writing the answers down?	**Qui va écrire les réponses?**
Me	**Moi**
You	**Toi**
Just a minute!	**Attends une minute!**
Well done!	**Bravo!**
Hurray!	**Youpee!**
Hard luck!	**Pas de chance!**
Never mind!	**Tant pis!**
It doesn't matter	**Ça ne fait rien**
Gosh!	**Oh là là!**
What!	**Quoi!**
Oh no!	**Oh non!**
That's right	**C'est juste**
That's wrong	**C'est faux**
Don't cheat!	**Ne triche pas!**
Hurry up!	**Dépêche-toi!**
Come on!	**Allez!**
Quickly!	**Vite!**
Great!	**Génial!**
Terrific!	**Terrible!**
Brilliant!	**Super!**
This is fun	**C'est amusant**
This is boring	**C'est barbant**
Could you lend me …?	**Tu peux me prêter …?**
Give me …	**Donne-moi …**
Pass me the …	**Passe-moi le/la/les …**

Language for classroom use: German

Language for teacher use

General classroom requests and instructions

Sit down	**Setz dich/Setzt euch**
Stand up	**Steh auf/Steht auf**
Switch the light on/off	**Mach das Licht an/aus**
Put up your hand	**Melde dich/Meldet euch**
Quiet, please!	**Ruhe, bitte!**
Have you finished?	**Bist du/Seid ihr fertig?**
Where is your ...?	**Wo ist dein/deine ...?**
Get out your ...	**Nimm deine/Nehmt eure ... heraus**
Please repeat	**Alle zusammen Wiederhol/Wiederholt, bitte!**
A volunteer, please	**Freiwillige, bitte**
Come here	**Komm/Kommt hierher!**
Do you understand?	**Verstehst du/Versteht ihr?**
Speak a bit louder	**Sprich/Sprecht etwas lauter**
Speak more quietly, please	**Sprich/Specht leiser, bitte**
Say it in ..., please	**Sag/Sagt es bitte auf ...**
Who would like to read?	**Wer möchte lesen?**
Try again	**Versuch's/Versucht's noch einmal**
Give out the books	**Verteil/Verteilt die Bücher**
Collect the books	**Sammle/Sammelt die Bücher ein**
Write down your homework	**Schreib/Schreibt die Hausaufgaben auf**
Give in your homework	**Gib deine/Gebt eure Hausaufgaben ab**
Learn for a test	**Lern/Lernt für einen Test**
Please open the window	**Mach bitte das Fenster auf**
Please close the window	**Mach bitte das Fenster zu**
Who got it right?	**Wer hat es richtig?**
Put your things away	**Packt eure Sachen ein**
Stand behind your chairs	**Stellt euch hinter den Stuhl**
Put up your chairs	**Stellt euren Stuhl hoch**
Stack your chairs	**Stapelt eure Stühle**
Put your bags on the floor	**Legt eure Taschen auf den Boden**
Sit in a circle	**Setz euch im Kreis hin**

Expressions of praise

Quite good	**Ganz gut**
Well done!	**Gut gemacht!**
Very good	**Sehr gut**
Excellent	**Ausgezeichnet**
Good try	**Gelungener Versuch**
Congratulations!	**Gratuliere!**
Not bad	**Nicht schlecht**
Much better	**Schon viel besser**
OK	**In Ordnung (Okay)**
Wonderful!	**Wunderbar!**
Brilliant!	**Hervorragend!**
Good idea	**Gute Idee**
Original	**Sehr originell**

Expressions of reprimand/criticism

Line up quietly	**Stellt euch leise hintereinander auf**
Take off your coat	**Zieh deinen/Zieht euren Mantel aus**
Be quiet	**Sei/Seid ruhig**
There is too much noise	**Es ist zu laut**
That's enough	**Jetzt reicht's**
Don't shout out	**Nicht dazwischenrufen**
Pay attention	**Paß/Paßt auf**

Calm down	**Beruhige dich/Beruhigt euch**
Don't be silly	**Hör/Hört auf mit dem Unsinn**
Are you chewing?	**Kaust du etwa?**
Put it in the bin	**Wirf es in den Papierkorb**
You can do better	**Das kannst du/könnt ihr besser**
Turn round	**Dreh dich/Dreht euch um**
Don't swing back on your chair	**Wackel nicht mit dem Stuhl**
Sit properly	**Setz dich/Setzt euch richtig hin**
Come back after school	**Komm nach dem Unterricht zu mir!**
Lines	**Strafarbeit**
Detention on … (day) at …	**Nachsitzen … um … Uhr**
Look this way	**Sieh/Seht hierher**

Instructions for activities

Find a partner	**Such/Sucht einen Partner**
Get into groups of …	**Setzt euch in (Vierer) gruppen**
Find page …	**Such/Sucht die Seite …**
Copy this into your books	**Schreibt das ab**
In the back of your books	**Hinten im Heft**
In the front of your books	**Vorne im Heft**
Write in the margin	**Schreib/Schreibt auf den Rand**
Write it in rough	**Schreib/Schreibt es vor**
Leave a line	**Laß/Laßt eine Zeile frei**
Swap books	**Tauscht eure hefte aus**
Fill in the grid	**Füll/Füllt die Tabelle aus**
Correct your work	**Berichtige deine/Berichtigt eure Arbeit**
Mark each other's work	**Korrigiert gegenseitig eure Arbeit**
Read this	**Lies/Lest das**
Draw and label	**Zeichne und beschrifte/Zeichnet und beschriftet**
Draw a picture	**Mal/Malt ein Bild**
Ask questions	**Stell/Stellt Fragen**
Answer the questions	**Beantworte/Beantwortet die Fragen**
Ask your partner	**Frag deinen/Fragt euren partner**
Don't let your partner see	**Nicht zeigen**
Cover this with your hand	**Deck/Deckt dies mit deiner/Eurer Hand ab**
Tick the boxes	**Kreuz an/Kreuzt an**
Copy the grid	**Schreib/Schreibt die Tabelle ab**
Fill in the gaps	**Füll/Füllt die Lücken aus**
Join up the words and the pictures	**Welche Wörter gehören zu den Bildern?**
Mix up the cards	**Misch/Mischt die Karten**
Look it up in the dictionary	**Sieh/Seht im Wörterbuch nach**
Pretend that you are …	**Du bist/Ihr seid jetzt …**
Mime	**Spiel/Spielt es**
Do the role-play	**Macht das Rollenspiel**
Have a conversation	**Unterhaltet euch**
Take it in turns	**Abwechselnd**
Imagine	**Stell dir/Stellt euch vor**
Think of	**Denk/Denkt an**
Whisper	**Flüster/Flüstert**
Team A, B, C	**Mannschaft/Gruppe A, B, C**
Stand in line	**Stellt euch hintereinander auf**
You have five minutes	**Du hast/Ihr habt fünf Minuten Zeit**
Start with …	**Fang/Fangt an mit …**
Rewind the cassette	**Spul/Spult die Kassette zurück**
Listen to the cassette	**Hör dir/Hört euch die Kassette an**
Record on cassette	**Nimm/Nehmt es auf**
Record on video	**Nimm/Nehmt es auf Video auf/Zeichne/Zeichnet es auf**
Put the disc in the disc drive	**Leg/Legt die Diskette ein**
Load the programme	**Lade/Ladet das Program**
Type in …	**Tipp/Tippt … ein**
Delete	**Lösch/Löscht**
Press	**Drück/Drückt**

| Save | Speicher/Speichert ab |
| Print your work | Druck deine/Druckt eure Arbeit aus |

Explanations (grammar)

Look at this	Sieh dir/Seht euch das an
Notice this	Beachte/Beachtet das
It's different	Es ist anders
It changes	Es ändert sich/Es verändert sich
It's important	Es ist wichtig
Take away this	Nimm/Nehmt dies weg
Put	Setz/Setzt
Don't forget	Nicht vergessen
It's masculine	Es ist männlich/maskulinum
It's feminine	Es ist weiblich/femininum
It's neuter	Es ist sächlich/neutrum
It begins with …	Es fängt mit … an
It ends with …	Es hört mit … auf
An ending	Eine Endung

Comments in exercise books

Good work	Gute Arbeit
Neat work	Ordentliche/Saubere Arbeit
Take more care	Gib dir meht Mühe
Too many mistakes	Zuviele Fehler
Too short	Zu kurz
Take more care with spellings	Achte mehr auf deine Rechtschreibung
Take more care with your handwriting	Achte mehr auf deine Handschrift
You can do better	Das kannst du besser
Good presentation	Saubere Ausführung
Where is your homework?	Wo sind deine Hausaufgaben?
See me!	Komm nach der Stunde zu mir!
Underline the title	Unterstreiche die Überschrift
Don't forget the date and title	Vergiß nicht Datum und Überschrift
Don't leave gaps	Laß keine Lücken
A big improvement	Eine deutliche Verbesserung
Write in sentences	Schreib in ganzen Sätzen
Don't write in English	Schreib nicht auf englisch
Copy with more care	Schreib sorgfältiger ab

Phrases for pupil use

To the teacher

Can you repeat that?	Können Sie das wiederholen?
Can you repeat that more slowly?	Können Sie das langsamer wiederholen?
How do you say … in …?	Wie sagt man … auf …?
What does … mean?	Was heißt/bedeutet …?
How do you spell …?	Wie schreibt man …?
I have (not) finished	Ich bin/Ich bin noch nicht fertig
I don't understand	Ich verstehe das nicht
I don't know	Ich weiß nicht
Is that right?	Ist das richtig?
Excuse me	Entschuldigung
Sorry	Es tut mir leid
Just a minute	Gleich/Einen Moment, bitte
I haven't got a …	Ich habe kein/keine/keinen …
I've forgotten my pen	Ich habe meinen Füller vergessen
I've forgotten my homework	Ich habe meine Hausaufgaben vergessen
May I have a piece of paper?	Ich möchte bitte ein Blatt Papier
What page is it?	Auf welcher Seite ist das?
Sorry I'm late	Entschuldigen Sie/Es tut mir leid, daß ich zu spät komme

May I go to the toilet?	**Darf ich auf Toilette gehen?**
May I leave?	**Darf ich gehen?**
May I go to my violin lesson?	**Darf ich zum Geigenunterricht?**
I feel ill	**Mir geht's nicht gut**
Can you help me?	**Können Sie mir helfen?**
I have a problem	**Ich habe ein Problem**
I didn't hear	**Ich habe es nicht gehört**
I can't see	**Ich kann es nicht sehen**
May I open the window?	**Darf ich das Fenster aufmachen/öffnen?**
May I close the window?	**Darf ich das Fenster zumachen/schließen?**
... is away	**... ist nicht da**
I was away	**Ich war nicht da**
Can you explain?	**Können sie das erklären?**
May I clean the board?	**Darf ich die Tafel wischen?**

Classroom objects

Book	**das Buch**
Exercise book	**das Heft**
Pen	**der Füller**
Biro	**der Kuli**
Pencil	**der Stift**
Rubber	**das Radiergummi**
Ruler	**das Lineal**
Scissors	**die Schere**
Glue	**der Kleber/Klebstoff**
Sellotape	**der Tesafilm**
Rough/scrap paper	**das Schmierpapier**
Compass	**der Zirkel**
Hole punch	**der Locher**
Highlighter	**der Textmarker**
Stapler	**der Hefter**
Drawing pin	**die Heftzwecke**
Paper clip	**die Büroklammer**
Calculator	**der (Taschen-) Rechner**
Felt-tip pen	**der Filzstift**
Pencil case	**die Federmappe/Federtasche**
Dictionary	**das Wörterbuch**
School bag	**die Schultasche/der Schulranzen**
Cassette	**die Kassette**
Tape recorder	**der Kassettenrekorder**
Listening centre	**der Kassettenrekorder mit mehreren Kopfhörern**
Headphones	**der Kopfhörer**
Video	**das Video**
Video player	**das Videogerät**
Video camera	**die Videokamera**
Television	**das Fernsehgerät/der Fernseher**
Computer	**der Computer**
Keyboard	**die Tastatur**
Screen	**der Bildschirm**
Disc	**die Diskette**
Disc drive	**das Laufwerk**
Printer	**der Drucker**
Concept keyboard	**die Bildtastatur**
Concept keyboard overlay	**die Befehlsleiste**
Blackboard	**die Tafel**
Chalk	**die Kreide**
Board rubber	**der Schwamm/der Lappen**
Whiteboard	**die Wand**
Whiteboard pen	**der Tafelschreiber/der Edding**
Overhead projector	**der Tageslichtprojektor/der Overheadprojektor**
Overhead transparency	**die Folie**
Projector	**der Projektor**

Games

Dice	**der Würfel**
Counter	**der Spielstein**
Cards	**die Karten**
Board	**das Spielbrett**
Shake the dice	**Würfel!**
Throw the dice	**Würfel!**
Go forward to …	**Geh/Geht vorwärts auf …**
Go back to …	**Geh/Geht zurück auf …**
Go back to the start	**Fang von vorne an**
Have another throw	**Würfle/Würfelt noch (ein)mal**
Odd / Even number	**Die ungerade/gerade Zahl**
The winner	**Der Sieger/Die Siegerin**
Guess	**Rate/Ratet**
Miss a turn	**Einmal aussetzen**
Turn over	**Dreh/Dreht um**
Deal out the cards	**Verteil/Verteilt die Karten**
Pick up a card	**Nimm/Nehmt eine Karte**
Collect pairs	**Sammle/Sammelt Paare**
Collect sets of …	**Sammle/Sammelt …**

Talking to each other

I'll start	**Ich fange an**
You can start	**Du kannst anfangen**
I'm person A	**Ich bin A**
You're person B	**Du bist B**
Whose turn is it?	**Wer ist dran?**
It's your turn	**Du bist dran**
It's my turn	**Ich bin dran**
What?	**Was?**
Can you repeat?	**Noch einmal, bitte**
Who's writing the answers down?	**Wer schreibt auf?**
Me	**Ich**
You	**Du**
Just a minute!	**Gleich/Moment!**
Well done!	**Gut gemacht!**
Hurray!	**Hurra/Juchu!**
Hard luck!	**Pech gehabt!**
Never mind!	**Macht nichts!**
It doesn't matter	**Das ist egal**
Gosh!	**Mann/Mensch!**
What!	**Was!**
Oh no!	**Oh nein/Ach, Mensch!**
That's right	**Das stimmt/Das ist richtig**
That's wrong	**Das stimmt nicht/Das ist falsch**
Don't cheat!	**Nicht schummeln!**
Hurry up!	**Mach schnell/Los!**
Come on!	**Mach schon!**
Quickly!	**Schnell!**
Great!	**Toll/Spitze!**
Terrific!	**Wahnsinn!**
Brilliant!	**Super**
This is fun	**Das macht Spaß**
This is boring	**Das ist langweilig**
Could you lend me …?	**Kannst du mir ein/eine/einen … leihen?**
Give me …	**Gib mir …**
Pass me the …	**Gib mir den/die/das …**

Language for classroom use: Italian

Language for teacher use

General classroom requests and instructions

Sit down	**Sedetevi**
Stand up	**Attenti/In piedi**
Switch the light on/off	**Accendi/Spegni la luce**
Put up your hand	**Alza/Alzate la mano**
Quiet, please	**Silenzio, per favore**
Have you finished?	**Hai finito?/Avete finito?**
Where is your ...?	**Dov'è il tuo/la tua ...?**
Get out your ...	**Prendi il tuo/la tua .../Prendete i vostri/le vostre ...**
Please repeat	**Ripeti/Ripetete, per favore**
All together	**Tutti insieme**
A volunteer, please	**Un volontario, per favore**
Come here	**Vieni/Venite qui**
Do you understand?	**Hai capito?/Avete capito?**
Speak a bit louder	**Parla/Parlate un po' più forte**
Speak more quietly, please	**Parla/Parlate un po' più piano, per favore**
Say it in..., please	**Dillo/Ditelo in ..., per favore**
Who would like to read?	**Chi vuole leggere?**
Try again	**Prova/Provate di nuovo**
Give out the books	**Distribuisci/Distribuite i libri**
Collect the books	**Raccogli/Raccogliete i libri**
Write down your homework	**Scrivi/Scrivete i compiti per la prossima volta**
Give in your homework	**Consegna il compito/Consegnate i compiti**
Learn for a test	**Impara/Imparate per il compito in classe**
Please open the window	**Per favore, apri la finestra**
Please close the window	**Per favore, chiudi la finestra**
Who got it right?	**Chi l'ha fatto giusto?**
Put your things away	**Mettete via tutto**
Stand behind your chairs	**In piedi dietro le sedie**
Put up your chairs	**Mettete le sedie sui banchi**
Stack your chairs	**Mettete le sedie l'una sull'altra**
Put your bags on the floor	**Mettete le cartelle per terra**
Sit in a circle	**Sedetevi formando un cerchio**

Expressions of praise

Quite good	**Abbastanza bene**
Well done!	**Bene**
Very good	**Benissimo**
Excellent	**Ottimo**
Good try	**Hai fatto del tuo meglio**
Congratulations!	**Complimenti!**
Not bad	**Non c'è male**
Much better	**Molto meglio**
OK	**OK/Discreto**
Wonderful!	**Meraviglioso!**
Brilliant!	**Fantastico!**
Good idea	**Buona idea**
Original	**Originale**

Expressions of reprimand/criticism

Line up quietly	**Mettetevi in fila, in silenzio**
Take off your coat	**Togliti/Toglietevi il cappotto**
Be quiet	**Sta zitto/a/State zitti**
There is too much noise	**C'è troppo chiasso**
That's enough	**Adesso basta**
Don't shout out	**Non urlare/urlate**

Pay attention	**Sta attento/a/State attenti**
Calm down	**Calmatevi/Calmati**
Don't be silly	**Non fare lo scemo**
Are you chewing?	**Cosa stai/state masticando?**
Put it in the bin	**Mettilo/Mettetelo nel cestino**
You can do better	**Puoi/Potete far meglio**
Turn round	**Girati/Giratevi**
Don't swing back on your chair	**Non ti dondolare con la sedia**
Sit properly	**Siediti/Sedetevi bene**
Come back after school	**Torna/Tornate dopo la scuola**
Lines	**Scrivi/Scrivete ... volte**
Detention on ... (day) at ...	**Punizione il (giorno) alle (ore)**
Look this way	**Guarda/Guardate qui**

Instructions for activities

Find a partner	**Scegli/Scegliete un compagno**
Get into groups of ...	**Formate gruppi di ...**
Find page ...	**Cerca/Cercate la pagina ...**
Copy this into your books	**Copiate sul quaderno**
In the back of your books	**Alla fine del quaderno**
In the front of your books	**All'inizio del quaderno**
Write in the margin	**Scrivi/Scrivete in margine**
Write it in rough	**Scrivi/Scrivete in brutta copia**
Leave a line	**Lascia/Lasciate un rigo**
Swap books	**Scambiatevi i quaderni**
Fill in the grid	**Completa/Completate il grafico**
Correct your work	**Correggi/Correggete i tuoi/vostri compiti**
Mark each other's work	**Correggetevi i compiti a vicenda**
Read this	**Leggi/Leggete questo**
Draw and label	**Disegna/Disegnate e scrivi/scrivete sotto che cos'è**
Draw a picture	**Fa/Fate un disegno**
Ask questions	**Fa/Fate delle domande**
Answer the questions	**Rispondi/Rispondete alle domande**
Ask your partner	**Chiedi/Chiedete al tuo/vostro compagno**
Don't let your partner see	**Non far/fate vedere al tuo/vostro compagno**
Cover this with your hand	**Copri/Coprite questo con la mano**
Tick the boxes	**Segna/Segnate la casella giusta**
Copy the grid	**Copia/Copiate il grafico**
Fill in the gaps	**Completa/Completate**
Join up the words and the pictures	**Unisci/Unite le parole con le figure**
Mix up the cards	**Mischia/Mischiate le carte**
Look it up in the dictionary	**Guarda/Guardate sul dizionario**
Pretend that you are ...	**Fingi/Fingete di essere ...**
Mime	**Mima/Mimate**
Do the role-play	**Fate questo role-play**
Have a conversation	**Conversate/Parlate tra di voi**
Take it in turns	**Fate a turno**
Imagine	**Immagina/Immaginate**
Think of	**Pensa/Pensate a**
Whisper	**Dillo/Ditelo sotto voce**
Team A, B, C	**Squadra A, B, C**
Stand in line	**Mettetevi in fila**
You have five minutes	**Hai/Avete cinque minuti**
Start with ...	**Comincia/Cominciate con ...**
Rewind the cassette	**Riavvolgi/Riavvolgete la cassetta**
Listen to the cassette	**Ascolta/Ascoltate la cassetta**
Record on cassette	**Registra/Registrate su cassetta**
Record on video	**Registra/Registrate sulla videocassetta**
Put the disc in the disc drive	**Metti/Mettete il dischetto nel disc-drive**
Load the programme	**Carica/caricate il programma**
Type in ...	**Immetti/Immettete/Digita/Digitate**
Delete	**Cancella/Cancellate**
Press	**Premi/Premete**

Save	Salva/Salvate
Print your work	Stampa/Stampate il lavoro

Explanations (grammar)

Look at this	Guarda/Guardate qui
Notice this	Nota/Notate questo
It's different	È diverso
It changes	Cambia
It's important	È importante
Take away this	Togli/Togliete questo
Put	Metti/Mettete
Don't forget	Non dimenticare/Non dimenticate
It's masculine	È maschile
It's feminine	È femminile
It's neuter	È neutro
It begins with ...	Comincia con ...
It ends with ...	Termina con ...
An ending	Una desinenza

Comments in exercise books

Good work	Un buon compito
Neat work	Ordinato
Take more care	Fa' più attenzione
Too many mistakes	Troppi errori
Too short	Troppo breve
Take more care with spellings	Sta più attento/a all'ortografia
Take more care with your handwriting	Scrivi meglio
You can do better	Puoi far meglio
Good presentation	Lavoro ordinato
Where is your homework?	Dov'è il tuo compito?
See me!	Devo parlarti
Underline the title	Sottolinea il titolo
Don't forget the date and title	Non dimenticare la data e il titolo
Don't leave gaps	Non lasciare spazi vuoti
A big improvement	Un deciso miglioramento
Write in sentences	Scrivi frasi complete
Don't write in English	Non scrivere in inglese
Copy with more care	Copia con più attenzione

Phrases for pupil use

To the teacher

Can you repeat that?	Lo può ripetere?
Can you repeat that more slowly?	Lo può ripetere più lentamente?
How do you say ... in ...?	Come si dice ... in ...?
What does ... mean?	Cosa vuol dire ...?
How do you spell ...?	Come si scrive ...?
I've/I haven't finished	Ho/Non ho finito
I don't understand	Non ho capito
I don't know	Non lo so
Is that right?	È giusto?
Excuse me	Mi scusi
Sorry	Mi dispiace
Just a minute	Un momento
I haven't got a ...	Non ho un/una ...
I've forgotten my pen	Ho dimenticato la penna
I've forgotten my homework	Ho dimenticato il compito a casa
May I have a piece of paper?	Posso avere un foglio?
What page is it?	A che pagina?
Sorry I'm late	Mi scusi il ritardo

May I go to the toilet?	**Posso andare in bagno?**
May I leave?	**Posso uscire?**
May I go to my violin lesson?	**Posso andare alla lezione di violino?**
I feel ill	**Mi sento male**
Can you help me?	**Mi può aiutare?**
I have a problem	**Ho un problema**
I didn't hear	**Non ho sentito**
I can't see	**Non vedo**
May I open the window?	**Posso aprire la finestra?**
May I close the window?	**Posso chiudere la finestra?**
... is away	**... è assente**
I was away	**Ero assente**
Can you explain?	**Può spiegare ...?**
May I clean the board?	**Posso cancellare la lavagna?**

Classroom objects

Book	**Il libro**
Exercise book	**Il quaderno**
Pen	**La penna**
Biro	**La biro**
Pencil	**La matita**
Rubber	**La gomma**
Ruler	**La riga**
Scissors	**Le forbici**
Glue	**La colla**
Sellotape	**Lo scotch/Il nastro adesivo**
Rough/scrap paper	**I fogli per la brutta copia**
Compass	**Il compasso**
Hole punch	**La perforatrice**
Highlighter	**L'evidenziatore**
Stapler	**La cucitrice/spillatrice**
Drawing pin	**La puntina da disegno**
Paper clip	**La graffetta**
Calculator	**Il calcolatore**
Felt-tip pen	**Il pennarello**
Pencil case	**Il portapenne/portamatite**
Dictionary	**Il dizionario**
School bag	**La borsa cartella**
Cassette	**La cassetta**
Tape recorder	**Il registratore**
Listening centre	**Il laboratorio linguistico**
Headphones	**La cuffia**
Video	**Il video**
Video player	**Il video registratore**
Video camera	**La videocamera**
Television	**La televisione**
Computer	**Il computer**
Keyboard	**La tastiera**
Screen	**Lo schermo**
Disc	**Il dischetto/floppy disc**
Disc drive	**Il disc-drive/l'unità dischi**
Printer	**La stampante**
Concept keyboard	**La tastiera dell'elaboratore**
Concept keyboard overlay	**La mascherina**
Blackboard	**La lavagna**
Chalk	**Il gesso**
Board rubber	**Il cancellino**
Whiteboard	**La lavagna bianca**
Whiteboard pen	**Il pennarello**
Overhead projector	**La lavagna luminosa**
Overhead transparency	**Il lucido**
Projector	**Il proiettore**

Games

Dice	**I dadi**
Counter	**La pedina**
Cards	**Le carte**
Board	**Il tabellone**
Shake the dice	**Scuoti/Scuotete i dadi**
Throw the dice	**Lancia/Lanciate i dadi**
Go forward to …	**Avanza/Avanzate a …**
Go back to …	**Torna/Tornate indietro a …**
Go back to the start	**Torna/Tornate alla partenza**
Have another throw	**Lancia/Lanciate di nuovo i dadi**
Odd/Even number	**Il numero dispari/pari**
The winner	**Il vincitore/La vincitrice**
Guess	**Indovina/Indovinate**
Miss a turn	**Sta fermo/a/State fermi un giro**
Turn over	**Gira/Girate**
Deal out the cards	**Fa/Fate le carte**
Pick up a card	**Prendi/Prendete una carta**
Collect pairs	**Trova/Trovate le coppie**
Collect sets of …	**Trova/Trovate i gruppi di …**

Talking to each other

I'll start	**Comincio io**
You can start	**Comincia tu**
I'm person A	**Io sono A**
You're person B	**Tu sei B**
Whose turn is it?	**A chi tocca?**
It's your turn	**Tocca a te**
It's my turn	**Tocca a me**
What?	**Come?/Che cosa?**
Can you repeat?	**Puoi ripetere?**
Who's writing the answers down?	**Chi sta scrivendo le risposte?**
Me	**Io**
You	**Tu**
Just a minute!	**Aspetta un minuto!**
Well done!	**Bravo/a!**
Hurray!	**Evviva!**
Hard luck!	**Ti è andata male!/Sei stato/a sfortunato/a!**
Never mind!	**Non importa!**
It doesn't matter	**Non fa niente**
Gosh!	**Accidenti!**
What!	**Come!**
Oh no!	**Oh no!**
That's right	**È giusto**
That's wrong	**È sbagliato**
Don't cheat!	**Non imbrogliare!**
Hurry up!	**Fai presto!**
Come on!	**Dai!**
Quickly!	**Sbrigati!**
Great!	**Stupendo!**
Terrific!	**Fantastico!**
Brilliant!	**Magnifico!**
This is fun	**È divertente**
This is boring	**È scocciante**
Could you lend me …?	**Mi puoi prestare …?**
Give me …	**Dammi …**
Pass me the …	**Passami il/la/lo …**

Language for classroom use: Russian

Language for teacher use

General classroom requests and instructions

Sit down	Садись, садитесь
Stand up	Встань, встаньте
Switch the light on/off	Включи, выключи свет
Put your hand up	Подними руку, поднимите руки
Quiet, please	Тихо, пожалуйста
Have you finished?	Ты закончил? Вы закончили?
Where is your...?	Где...?
Get out your...	Достань...Достаньте...
Please repeat	Повтори, повторите, пожалуйста
All together	Все вместе
A volunteer, please	Доброволец (сделать что-либо), пожалуйста
Come here	Подойди, подойдите сюда
Do you understand?	Понятно?
Speak a bit louder	Говори, говорите погромче
Speak more quietly, please	Говори, говорите потише, пожалуйста
Say it in Russian, please	По-русски, пожалуйста
Who would like to read?	Кто хочет почитать?/прочитать (что-либо)?
Try again	Попробуй, попробуйте ещё раз
Give out the books	Раздай, раздайте учебники/тетради
Collect the books	Собери, соберите учебники/тетради
Write down your homework	Запиши, запишите домашнее задание
Give in your homework	Сдай, сдайте домашнее задание
Learn for a test	Выучите (что-либо) к контрольной работе
Please open the window	Пожалуйста, открой окно
Please close the window	Пожалуйста, закрой окно
Who got it right?	Кто правильно ответил? (сделал? написал?)
Put your things away	Соберите вещи
Stand behind your chairs	Встаньте за стульями
Put up your chairs	Поставьте стулья на столы/парты
Stack your chairs	Соберите стулья
Put your bags on the floor	Положите сумки на пол
Sit in a circle	Сядьте в круг

Expressions of praise

Quite good	Довольно хорошо
Well done	Молодец
Very good	Очень хорошо
Excellent	Отлично
Good try	Хорошая попытка
Congratulations!	Поздравляю!
Not bad	Неплохо
Much better	Гораздо лучше
OK	Хорошо
Wonderful!	Чудесно!
Brilliant!	Блестяще!
Good idea	Хорошая мысль
Original	Оригинально

Expressions of reprimand/criticism

Line up quietly	Стойте смирно
Take off your coats	Сними, снимите пальто
Be quiet	Тихо
There is too much noise	Очень шумно
That's enough	Довольно
Don't shout out	Не кричи, не кричите
Pay attention	Обрати, обратите внимание
Calm down	Успокойся, успокойтесь
Don't be silly	Не валяй (не валяйте) дурака
Are you chewing?	Ты жуёшь (жвачку)?
Put it in the bin	Брось в мусорное ведро
You can do better	Ты мог бы (вы могли бы) сделать получше
Turn around	Повернись, повернитесь (к доске)
Don't swing back on your chair	Не раскачивайся на стуле
Sit properly	Сядь (сядьте), как следует
Come back after school	Подойди ко мне после уроков
Lines	Письменное наказание
Detention on...(day) at...(time)	Задержание после уроков в... в...
Look this way	Посмотри, посмотрите сюда

Instructions for activities

Find a partner	Найди, найдите партнёра
Get into groups of...	Разделитесь на группы по...(шесть человек)
Find page...	Открой, откройте на странице...
Copy this into your books	Перепишите (что-либо) в тетради
In the back of your books	На последней странице
In the front of your books	На первой странице
Write in the margin	Напиши, напишите на полях
Write in rough	Напиши, напишите в черновике
Leave a line	Пиши, пишите через строчку
Swap books	Поменяйся, поменяйтесь тетрадями
Fill in the grid	Заполни, заполните таблицу
Correct your work	Проверь, проверьте работу
Mark each other's work	Проверьте работу соседа
Read this	Прочитай, прочитайте
Draw and label	Нарисуй (нарисуйте) и напиши (напишите)
Draw a picture	Нарисуй, нарисуйте картину
Ask questions	Задай, задайте вопросы
Answer the questions	Ответь, ответьте на вопросы
Ask your partner	Спроси, спросите партнёра
Don't let your partner see	Проверь (проверьте), чтобы партнёр не видел
Cover this with your hand	Закрой (закройте) это ладонью
Tick the boxes	Отметь (отметьте) галочкой квадратики
Copy the grid	Срисуй, срисуйте таблицу
Fill in the gaps	Заполни, заполните пропуски
Join up the words and the pictures	Соедини (соедините) стрелочкой картинки со словами
Mix up the cards	Перемешай, перемешайте карточки
Look it up in the dictionary	Смотри, смотрите в словаре
Pretend that you are...	Представь, что ты...; представьте, что вы...
Mime	Изобрази (изобразите) жестами
Do the role-play	Разыграйте по ролям
Have a conversation	Разыграйте диалог
Take it in turns	По очереди
Imagine	Представь, представьте
Think of...	Придумай (придумайте) что-либо
Whisper	Прошепчи, прошепчите

Team A, B, C	Кома́нды А, Б, В
Stand in line	Вста́ньте в о́чередь
You have five minutes	У вас (тебя́) есть пять мину́т
Start with...	Начни́, начни́те с (чего́-либо)
Rewind the cassette	Перемота́й (перемота́йте) кассе́ту
Listen to the cassette	Послу́шай (послу́шайте) кассе́ту
Record on cassette	Запиши́ (запиши́те) на кассе́ту
Record on video	Запиши́ (запиши́те) на ви́део
Put the disc in the disc drive	Вста́вь (вста́вьте) диске́ту в дисково́д
Load the programme	Запусти́, запусти́те програ́мму
Type in...	Напеча́тай, напеча́тайте...
Delete	Сбро́сь, сбро́сьте
Press	Нажми́, нажми́те
Save	Сохрани́, сохрани́те
Print your work	Напеча́тай твою́ рабо́ту/напеча́тайте ва́шу рабо́ту

Explanations (grammar)

Look at this	Посмотри́, посмотри́те на (что́-либо)
Notice this	Обрати́, обрати́те внима́ние на (что́-либо)
It's different	Э́то сло́во пи́шется по-друго́му
It changes	Э́то сло́во изменя́ется
It's important	Э́то ва́жный моме́нт
Take away this	Отбро́сь; сотри́ (отбро́сьте; сотри́те)
Put	Вста́вь, вста́вьте
Don't forget	Не забу́дь, не забу́дьте
It's masculine	Э́то мужско́й род
It's feminine	Э́то же́нский род
It's neuter	Э́то сре́дний род
It begins with...	Сло́во начина́ется с бу́квы...
It ends with...	Сло́во ока́нчивается на бу́кву...
An ending	Оконча́ние

Comments in exercise books

Good work	Хоро́шая рабо́та
Neat work	Аккура́тная рабо́та
Take more care	Будь бо́лее внима́телен
Too many mistakes	Сли́шком мно́го оши́бок
Too short	Сли́шком ма́ло
Take more care with spelling	Будь внима́тельнее с орфогра́фией
Take more care with your handwriting	Пиши́ аккура́тнее
You can do better	Ты мог бы сде́лать полу́чше
Good presentation	Аккура́тная/приле́жная рабо́та
Where is your homework?	Где твоя́ дома́шняя рабо́та?
See me!	Подойди́ ко мне по́сле уро́ка
Underline the title	Подчеркни́ те́му уро́ка по лине́йке
Don't forget the date and title	Не забу́дь записа́ть число́ и те́му
Don't leave gaps	Не оставля́й про́пусков
A big improvement	Гора́здо лу́чше
Write in sentences	Соста́вь по́лные предложе́ния
Don't write in English	Не пиши́ по-англи́йски
Copy with more care	Спиши́ внима́тельнее

Phrases for pupil use

To the teacher

Can you repeat that?	Повторите, пожалуйста
Can you repeat that more slowly?	Повторите помедленнее, пожалуйста
How do you say...in Russian?	Как по-русски...?
What does...mean?	Что значит...?
How do you spell...?	Как пишется...?
I've/I've not finished	Я (не) закончил
I don't understand	Я не понимаю
I don't know	Я не знаю
Is that right?	Это правильно?
Excuse me	Извините
Sorry	Извините
Just a minute	Минуточку
I haven't got a...	У меня нет...(чего-либо)
I've forgotten my pen	Я забыл ручку
I have forgotten my homework	Я забыл домашнюю работу
May I have a piece of paper?	Дайте мне, пожалуйста, лист бумаги
What page is it?	На какой это странице?
Sorry I'm late...	Извините, что я опоздал(а)
May I go to the toilet?	Можно выйти?
May I leave?	Можно выйти?
May I go to my violin lesson?	Можно идти на занятие по скрипке?
I feel ill	Я неважно себя чувствую
Can you help me?	Вы не могли бы мне помочь?
I have a problem	У меня есть проблема
I didn't hear	Я не расслышал(а)
I can't see	Мне не видно
May I open the window?	Можно открыть окно?
May I close the window?	Можно закрыть окно?
...is away	(кого) нет; отсутствует (кто)
I was away	Меня не было; я отсутствовал(а)
Can you explain...?	Объясните, пожалуйста...
May I clean the board?	Мне можно стереть с доски?

Classroom objects

Book	Книга; учебник
Exercise book	Тетрадь
Pen	Ручка
Biro	Шариковая ручка
Pencil	Карандаш
Rubber	Ластик
Ruler	Линейка
Scissors	Ножницы
Glue	Клей
Sellotape	Скотч
Rough/scrap paper	Черновик
Compass	Циркуль
Hole punch	Дырокол
Highlighter	Люминисцентный фломастер
Stapler	Скоросшиватель; степлер
Drawing pin	Кнопка
Paper clip	Скрепка
Calculator	Калькулятор
Felt-tip pen	Фломастер
Pencil case	Пенал

Dictionary	Словарь
School bag	Школьная сумка
Cassette	Кассета
Tape recorder	Магнитофон
Listening centre	Аудиоцентр; лингафонный уголок
Headphones	Наушинки
Video	Видео
Video player	Видеоплеер
Video camera	Видеокамера
Television	Телевизор
Computer	Компьютер
Keyboard	Клавиатура
Screen	Экран
Disc	Дискета
Disc drive	Дисковод
Printer	Принтер
Concept keyboard	Понятийная клавиатура
Concept keyboard overlay	Оверлей для понятийной клавиатуры
Blackboard	Доска
Chalk	Мел
Board rubber	Щётка (для доски)
Whiteboard	Белая доска
Whiteboard pen	Фломастер (для белой доски)
Overhead projector	Кодоскоп
Overhead transparency	Плёнка (для кодоскопа)
Projector	Проектор

Games

Dice	Кости
Counter	Фишка
Cards	Карты
Board	Поле
Shake the dice	Встряхни, встряхните кости
Throw the dice	Брось, бросьте кости
Go forward to...	Вперёд на...
Go back to...	Назад на...
Go back to the start	Обрато на старт
Have another throw	Брось, бросьте (кости) ещё раз
Odd/Even number	Нечётное/чётное число
The winner	Победитель
Guess	Отгадай, отгадайте
Miss a turn	Пропусти, пропустите ход
Turn over	Переверни, переверните
Deal out the cards	Раздай, раздайте карты
Pick up a card	Возьми, возьмите карту
Collect pairs	Собери, соберите пары
Collect sets of...	Собери, соберите карточки (чего-либо; с чем-либо)

Talking to each other

I'll start	Я начну
You can start	Ты начинай
I'm person A	Я - <<А>>
You're person B	Ты - <<Б>>
Whose turn is it?	Чья очередь?
It's your turn	Твоя очередь
It's my turn	Моя очередь

What?	Что?
Can you repeat?	Повтори́
Who's writing the answers down?	Кто пи́шет отве́ты?
Me	Я
You	Ты
Just a minute	Мину́точку
Well done!	Молоде́ц!
Hurrah!	Ура́!
Hard luck!	Не везёт!
Never mind!	Ничего́!
It doesn't matter	Всё равно́
Gosh!	Ой!
What!	Что!
Oh no!	Ах, нет!
That's right	Пра́вильно
That's wrong	Непра́вильно
Don't cheat!	Не подсма́тривай; не ху́льничай!
Hurry up!	Скоре́е! Поспеши́!
Come on!	Дава́й!
Quickly!	Бы́стро!
Great!	Прекра́сно!
Terrific!	Замеча́тельно!
Brilliant!	Блестя́ще!
This is fun	Здо́рово
This is boring	Ску́чно
Could you lend me...?	Дай, пожа́луйста...
Give me...	Дай, пожа́луйста...
Pass me the...	Переда́й мне, пожа́луйста...

Language for classroom use: Spanish

Language for teacher use

General classroom requests and instructions

Sit down	**Siéntate/Sentaos**
Stand up	**Levánte/Levantaos**
Switch the light on/off	**Pon/Apaga la luz**
Put up your hand	**Levanta/Levantad la mano**
Quiet, please	**Silencio, por favor**
Have you finished?	**¿Has/Habéis terminado?**
Where is your ...?	**¿Dónde está tu ...?**
Get out your ...	**Saca tu(s) .../Sacad vuestro/a(s) ...**
Please repeat	**Repite/Repetid, por favor**
All together	**Todos juntos**
A volunteer, please	**Un voluntario, por favor**
Come here	**Ven/Venid aquí**
Do you understand?	**¿Entiendes/Entendéis?**
Speak a bit louder	**Habla/Hablad más alto**
Speak more quietly, please	**Habla/Hablad más bajo, por favor**
Say it in..., please	**Dilo/Decidlo en ..., por favor**
Who would like to read?	**¿Quién quiere leer?**
Try again	**Inténtalo/Intentadlo de nuevo**
Give out the books	**Reparte/Repartid los libros**
Collect the books	**Recoge/Recoged los libros**
Write down your homework	**Escribe/Escribid los deberes**
Give in your homework	**Dame/Dadme los deberes**
Learn for a test	**Apréndelo/Aprendedlo para un examen**
Please open the window	**Abre la ventana, por favor**
Please close the window	**Cierra la ventana, por favor**
Who got it right?	**¿Quién lo tiene bien?**
Put your things away	**Guardad las cosas**
Stand behind your chairs	**Poneos de pie detrás de la sillas**
Put up your chairs	**Subid las sillas**
Stack your chairs	**Apilad las sillas**
Put your bags on the floor	**Poned las bolsas en el suelo**
Sit in a circle	**Sentaos en círculo**

Expressions of praise

Quite good	**Bastante bien**
Well done!	**Bien hecho**
Very good	**Muy bien**
Excellent	**Sobresaliente**
Good try	**¡Así se trabaja!**
Congratulations!	**¡Te/Os felicito!**
Not bad	**No está mal**
Much better	**Mucho mejor**
OK	**Vale**
Wonderful!	**¡Maravilloso!**
Brilliant!	**¡Excelente!**
Good idea	**Buena idea**
Original	**Original**

Expressions of reprimand/criticism

Line up quietly	**Poneos en fila en silencio**
Take off your coat	**Quítate/Quitaos el abrigo**
Be quiet	**Cállate/Callaos**
There is too much noise	**Hay demasiado ruido**
That's enough	**Basta**
Don't shout out	**No grites/No gritéis**

Pay attention	**Presta/Prestad atención**
Calm down	**Cálmate/Calmaos**
Don't be silly	**Ne te pongas tonto/a**
Are you chewing?	**¿Estás/Estáis comiendo?**
Put it in the bin	**Ponlo/Ponedlo en la papelera**
You can do better	**Puedes/Podéis hacerlo mejor**
Turn round	**Date/Daos la vuelta**
Don't swing back on your chair	**No te balancees con la silla**
Sit properly	**Siéntate/Sentaos bien**
Come back after school	**Vuelve/Volved después del colegio**
Lines	**Copiar**
Detention on … (day) at …	**Castigado/a el … a las …**
Look this way	**Mira/Mirad por aquí**

Instructions for activities

Find a partner	**Encuentra/Encontrad una pareja**
Get into groups of …	**Formad grupos de …**
Find page …	**Busca/Buscad la página …**
Copy this into your books	**Copiad esto en vuestros cuadernos**
In the back of your books	**Al final del libro**
In the front of your books	**Al principio del libro**
Write in the margin	**Escribe/Escribid en el margen**
Write it in rough	**Escríbelo/Escribidlo en sucio**
Leave a line	**Deja/Dejad un espacio**
Swap books	**Cambia/Cambiad los libros**
Fill in the grid	**Rellena/Rellenad los cuadros**
Correct your work	**Corrige tu trabajo/Corregid vuestro trabajo**
Mark each other's work	**Corregid el trabajo de otra persona**
Read this	**Lee/Leed esto**
Draw and label	**Dibuja/Dibujad esto y pon/poned el nombre**
Draw a picture	**Haz/Haced un dibujo**
Ask questions	**Haz/Haced preguntas**
Answer the questions	**Contesta/Contestad a las preguntas**
Ask your partner	**Pregunta/Preguntad a tu/vuestro/a compañero/a**
Don't let your partner see	**No dejes/dejéis ver a tu/vuestro/a compañero/a**
Cover this with your hand	**Tápalo/Tapadlo con la mano**
Tick the boxes	**Marca/Marcad los recuadros**
Copy the grid	**Copia/Copiad los cuadros**
Fill in the gaps	**Rellena/Rellenad los espacios**
Join up the words and the pictures	**Haz/Haced corresponder las palabras con los dibujos**
Mix up the cards	**Mezcla/Mezclad las cartas**
Look it up in the dictionary	**Búscalo/Buscadlo en el diccionario**
Pretend that you are …	**Haced como si estás/estáis …**
Mime	**Haz/Haced mímica**
Do the role-play	**Haced el juego de roles**
Have a conversation	**Haced una conversación**
Take it in turns	**Hacedlo en turnos**
Imagine	**Imagina/Imaginad**
Think of …	**Piensa/Pensad en …**
Whisper	**Susurra/Susurrad**
Team A, B, C	**Equipo A, B, C**
Stand in line	**Poneos en fila**
You have five minutes	**Tienes/Tenéis cinco minutos**
Start with …	**Empieza/Empezad con …**
Rewind the cassette	**Rebobina/Rebobinad la cinta**
Listen to the cassette	**Escucha/Escuchad la cinta**
Record on cassette	**Graba/Grabad en la cinta**
Record on video	**Graba/Grabad en vídeo**
Put the disc in the disc drive	**Pon/Poned el disco en la unidad de discos**
Load the programme	**Carga/Cargad el programa**
Type in …	**Teclea/Teclead …**
Delete	**Borra/Borrad**
Press	**Apreta/Apretad**

Save	**Archiva/Archivad**
Print your work	**Imprime/Imprimid tu/vuestro trabajo**

Explanations (grammar)

Look at this	**Mira/Mirad esto**
Notice this	**Nota/Notad esto**
It's different	**Es diferente/distinto**
It changes	**Cambia**
It's important	**Es importante**
Take away this	**Quita/Quitad esto**
Put	**Pon/Poned**
Don't forget	**No olvides/No olvidéis**
It's masculine	**Es masculino**
It's feminine	**Es femenina**
It's neuter	**Es neutro**
It begins with …	**Empieza con …**
It ends with …	**Termina con …**
An ending	**Una terminación**

Comments in exercise books

Good work	**Buen trabajo**
Neat work	**Lo has hecho con cuidado**
Take more care	**Ten cuidado**
Too many mistakes	**Demasiados errores**
Too short	**Demasiado breve**
Take more care with spellings	**Ciudado con la ortografía**
Take more care with your handwriting	**Cuidado con la escritura**
You can do better	**Lo puedes hacer mejor**
Good presentation	**Buena presentación**
Where is your homework?	**¿Dónde están tus deberes?**
See me!	**¡Ven a verme!**
Underline the title	**Subraya el título**
Don't forget the date and title	**No olvides la fecha y el título**
Don't leave gaps	**No dejes espacios**
A big improvement	**Mucho mejor**
Write in sentences	**Escribe oraciones**
Don't write in English	**No escribas en inglés**
Copy with more care	**Copia con más cuidado**

Phrases for pupil use

To the teacher

Can you repeat that?	**¿Puedes Vd. repetir eso?**
Can you repeat that more slowly?	**¿Puedes Vd. repetirlo más lentamente?**
How do you say … in …?	**¿Cómo se dice … en … ?**
What does … mean?	**¿Qué quiere decir …? ¿Qué significa …?**
How do you spell …?	**¿Cómo se escribe …?**
I've/I haven't finished	**He/No he terminado**
I don't understand	**No entiendo**
I don't know	**No sé**
Is that right?	**¿Está bien?**
Excuse me	**Por favor**
Sorry	**Perdón**
Just a minute	**Un minuto**
I haven't got a …	**No tengo …**
I've forgotten my pen	**He olvidado el bolígrafo**
I've forgotten my homework	**He olvidado mis deberes**
May I have a piece of paper?	**¿Puedes Vd. darme un papel?**
What page is it?	**¿Qué página es?**
Sorry I'm late	**Lo siento, llego tarde**

May I go to the toilet?	**¿Puedo ir al retrete?**
May I leave?	**¿Puedo irme?**
May I go to my violin lesson?	**¿Puedo ir a mi clase de violín?**
I feel ill	**Me siento enfermo/a/No me encuentro bien**
Can you help me?	**¿Puedes ayudarme?**
I have a problem	**Tengo un problema**
I didn't hear	**No lo he oído**
I can't see	**No puedo ver**
May I open the window?	**¿Puedo abrir la ventana?**
May I close the window?	**¿Puede cerrar la ventana?**
… is away	**… no está**
I was away	**No estaba**
Can you explain?	**¿Puede explicar …?**
May I clean the board?	**¿Puedo borrar la pizarra?**

Classroom objects

Book	**El libro**
Exercise book	**El cuaderno**
Pen	**La pluma**
Biro	**El bolígrafo**
Pencil	**El lápiz**
Rubber	**La goma de borrar**
Ruler	**La regla**
Scissors	**Las tijeras**
Glue	**La goma**
Sellotape	**El scotch/El celo**
Rough/scrap paper	**En borrador/Pedazos de papel**
Compass	**El compás**
Hole punch	**El taladro**
Highlighter	**El rotulador fluorescente**
Stapler	**La grapadora**
Drawing pin	**La chincheta**
Paper clip	**El sujetapapeles/El clip**
Calculator	**La calculadora**
Felt-tip pen	**El rotulador**
Pencil case	**El estuche**
Dictionary	**El diccionario**
School bag	**La cartera**
Cassette	**La cinta**
Tape recorder	**La grabadora**
Listening centre	**La fonoteca**
Headphones	**Los cascos**
Video	**La cinta de vídeo**
Video player	**El vídeo**
Video camera	**La videocámara**
Television	**La televisión**
Computer	**El ordenador**
Keyboard	**El teclado**
Screen	**La pantalla**
Disc	**El disco**
Disc drive	**La unidad de discos**
Printer	**La impresora**
Concept keyboard	**El teclado tactil**
Concept keyboard overlay	**La hoja para un teclado tactil**
Blackboard	**La pizarra**
Chalk	**La tiza**
Board rubber	**El borrador**
Whiteboard	**La pizarra 'velleda'**
Whiteboard pen	**El rotulador pizarra 'velleda'**
Overhead projector	**El retroproyector**
Overhead transparency	**La transparencia**
Projector	**El proyector**

Games

Dice	**El dado**
Counter	**La ficha**
Cards	**Las cartas**
Board	**El tablero**
Shake the dice	**Agita/Agitad el dado**
Throw the dice	**Tira/Tirad el dado**
Go forward to …	**Avanza/Avanzad hasta …**
Go back to …	**Vuelve/Volved a …**
Go back to the start	**Vuelve/Volved al principio**
Have another throw	**Tira/Tirad otra vez**
Odd/Even number	**El número impar/par**
The winner	**El ganador/La ganadora**
Guess	**Adivina/Adivinad**
Miss a turn	**Pierdes/Perdéis un turno**
Turn over	**Vuelve/Volved las cartas**
Deal out the cards	**Reparte/Repartid las cartas**
Pick up a card	**Coge/Coged una carta**
Collect pairs	**Colecciona/Coleccionad parejas**
Collect sets of …	**Colecciona/Coleccionad grupos/familias de …**

Talking to each other

I'll start	**Empiezo yo**
You can start	**Puedes empezar**
I'm person A	**Soy la persona A**
You're person B	**Eres la persona B**
Whose turn is it?	**¿A quién le toca?**
It's your turn	**Te toca a ti?**
It's my turn	**Me toca a mí**
What?	**¿Qué?**
Can you repeat?	**¿Puedes repetir?**
Who's writing the answers down?	**¿Quién escribe las respuestas?**
Me	**Yo**
You	**Tú**
Just a minute!	**¡Un minuto!**
Well done!	**¡Bien hecho!**
Hurray!	**¡Bien!**
Hard luck!	**¡Mala suerte!**
Never mind!	**¡Es igual!**
It doesn't matter	**No importa**
Gosh!	**¡Oh, dios mío!/¡Cielos!/¡Vaya!**
What!	**¡Qué!**
Oh no!	**¡Ah, no!**
That's right	**Está bien**
That's wrong	**Está mal**
Don't cheat!	**¡No hagas trampas!**
Hurry up!	**¡Date prisa!**
Come on!	**¡Vamos!**
Quickly!	**¡Pronto!**
Great!	**¡Estupendo!**
Terrific!	**¡Fenomenal!**
Brilliant!	**¡Genial!**
This is fun	**Es divertido**
This is boring	**Es aburrido**
Could you lend me …?	**¿Puedes prestarme …?**
Give me …	**Dame …**
Pass me the …	**Pásame el/la/los/las …**

Language for classroom use

Language for teacher use

General classroom requests and instructions

Sit down
Stand up
Switch the light on/off
Put up your hand
Quiet, please
Have you finished?
Where is your ...?
Get out your ...
Please repeat
All together
A volunteer, please
Come here
Do you understand?
Speak a bit louder
Speak more quietly, please
Say it in..., please
Who would like to read?
Try again
Give out the books
Collect the books
Write down your homework
Give in your homework
Learn for a test
Please open the window
Please close the window
Who got it right?
Put your things away
Stand behind your chairs
Put up your chairs
Stack your chairs
Put your bags on the floor
Sit in a circle

Expressions of praise

Quite good
Well done!
Very good
Excellent
Good try
Congratulations!
Not bad
Much better
OK
Wonderful!
Brilliant!
Good idea
Original

Expressions of reprimand/criticism

Line up quietly
Take off your coat
Be quiet
There is too much noise
That's enough
Don't shout out

Pay attention
Calm down
Don't be silly
Are you chewing?
Put it in the bin
You can do better
Turn round
Don't swing back on your chair
Sit properly
Come back after school
Lines
Detention on ... (day) at ...
Look this way

Instructions for activities

Find a partner
Get into groups of ...
Find page ...
Copy this into your books
In the back of your books
In the front of your books
Write in the margin
Write it in rough
Leave a line
Swap books
Fill in the grid
Correct your work
Mark each other's work
Read this
Draw and label
Draw a picture
Ask questions
Answer the questions
Ask your partner
Don't let your partner see
Cover this with your hand
Tick the boxes
Copy the grid
Fill in the gaps
Join up the words and the pictures
Mix up the cards
Look it up in the dictionary
Pretend that you are ...
Mime
Do the role-play
Have a conversation
Take it in turns
Imagine
Think of ...
Whisper
Team A, B, C
Stand in line
You have five minutes
Start with ...
Rewind the cassette
Listen to the cassette
Record on cassette
Record on video
Put the disc in the disc drive
Load the programme
Type in ...
Delete
Press

Save
Print your work

Explanations (grammar)

Look at this
Notice this
It's different
It changes
It's important
Take away this
Put
Don't forget
It's masculine
It's feminine
It's neuter
It begins with ...
It ends with ...
An ending

Comments in exercise books

Good work
Neat work
Take more care
Too many mistakes
Too short
Take more care with spellings
Take more care with your
handwriting
You can do better
Good presentation
Where is your homework?
See me!
Underline the title
Don't forget the date and title
Don't leave gaps
A big improvement
Write in sentences
Don't write in English
Copy with more care

Phrases for pupil use

To the teacher

Can you repeat that?
Can you repeat that more slowly?
How do you say ... in ...?
What does ... mean?
How do you spell ...?
I've/I haven't finished
I don't understand
I don't know
Is that right?
Excuse me
Sorry
Just a minute
I haven't got a ...
I've forgotten my pen
I've forgotten my homework
May I have a piece of paper?
What page is it?
Sorry I'm late

May I go to the toilet?
May I leave?
May I go to my violin lesson?
I feel ill
Can you help me?
I have a problem
I didn't hear
I can't see
May I open the window?
May I close the window?
… is away
I was away
Can you explain?
May I clean the board?

Classroom objects

Book
Exercise book
Pen
Biro
Pencil
Rubber
Ruler
Scissors
Glue
Sellotape
Rough/scrap paper
Compass
Hole punch
Highlighter
Stapler
Drawing pin
Paper clip
Calculator
Felt-tip pen
Pencil case
Dictionary
School bag
Cassette
Tape recorder
Listening centre
Headphones
Video
Video player
Video camera
Television
Computer
Keyboard
Screen
Disc
Disc drive
Printer
Concept keyboard
Concept keyboard overlay
Blackboard
Chalk
Board rubber
Whiteboard
Whiteboard pen
Overhead projector
Overhead transparency
Projector

Games

Dice
Counter
Cards
Board
Shake the dice
Throw the dice
Go forward to …
Go back to …
Go back to the start
Have another throw
Odd/Even number
The winner
Guess
Miss a turn
Turn over
Deal out the cards
Pick up a card
Collect pairs
Collect sets of …

Talking to each other

I'll start
You can start
I'm person A
You're person B
Whose turn is it?
It's your turn
It's my turn
What?
Can you repeat?
Who's writing the answers down?
Me
You
Just a minute!
Well done!
Hurray!
Hard luck!
Never mind!
It doesn't matter
Gosh!
What!
Oh no!
That's right
That's wrong
Don't cheat!
Hurry up!
Come on!
Quickly!
Great!
Terrific!
Brilliant!
This is fun
This is boring
Could you lend me …?
Give me …
Pass me the …